Let's Get

CHINESE

Over **100** mouth-watering dishes

igloobooks

igloobooks

Published in 2017
by Igloo Books Ltd
Cottage Farm
Sywell
NN6 0BJ
www.igloobooks.com

Designed by Nicholas Gage
Edited by Jasmin Peppiatt

All imagery © iStock / Getty Images

LEO002 0717
2 4 6 8 10 9 7 5 3 1
ISBN 978-1-78557-445-0

Printed and manufactured in China

Contents

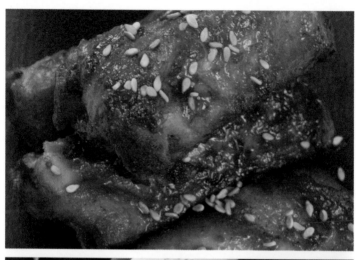

Meat Dishes

Stir-fried Beef with Crunchy Vegetables

2 tbsp vegetable oil
1 clove of garlic, squashed
1 sirloin steak, thinly sliced
2 tbsp dark soy sauce
1 small red onion, cut into wedges
1 small carrot, peeled and sliced diagonally
1 small red pepper, deseeded and sliced
1 small yellow pepper, deseeded and sliced
½ head broccoli, cut into florets
100 g / 3 ½ oz / ⅔ cup green beans,
 trimmed and halved
100 g / 3 ½ oz / ⅔ cup mangetout
1 pak choi, sliced
75 ml / 2 ½ fl. oz / ⅓ cup shaoxing rice wine

1. Heat the oil in a large wok and stir fry the garlic for 2 minutes. Remove with a slotted spoon and discard.
2. Add the steak and stir-fry for 4 minutes or until it starts to colour. Pour in the soy sauce and stir-fry until it has coated the beef and almost evaporated.
3. Add the onion and carrot and stir-fry over a high heat for 1 minute. Add the peppers and broccoli and stir-fry for 1 minute. Add the green beans, mangetout and pak choi and stir-fry for 1 minute.
4. Pour in the rice wine and stir-fry for 2 minutes, then serve immediately.

Chicken Curry

50 g / 1 ¾ oz / ¼ cup butter
30 g / 1 oz / ¼ cup plain (all-purpose) flour
2 tsp madras curry powder
2 tsp Chinese five spice powder
1 tsp ground ginger
1 tsp garlic powder
500 ml / 17 ½ fl. oz / 2 cups chicken stock
2 tbsp vegetable oil
2 cloves of garlic, crushed
1 tbsp fresh root ginger, finely chopped
3 skinless chicken breasts, cut into bite-
 sized pieces
1 onion, diced
1 red pepper, deseeded and sliced
steamed rice, to serve
flat-leaf parsley, to garnish

1. Firstly, make the sauce. Melt the butter in a saucepan, then stir in the flour, curry powder and spices. Stir over a gentle heat for 2 minutes, then gradually incorporate the stock. Continue stirring until the mixture simmers and thickens, then take the pan off the heat.
2. Heat the vegetable oil in a large wok and stir-fry the garlic and ginger for 1 minute. Add the chicken and stir-fry for 3 minutes or until opaque on the outside.
3. Add the onion and peppers and stir-fry for 2 minutes, then pour in the curry sauce.
4. Simmer for 4 minutes, stirring regularly, or until the chicken is cooked through.
5. Serve the curry on a bed of steamed rice, garnished with parsley.

SERVES: 4 | PREP TIME: 30 MINS | COOKING TIME: 4 MINS

Sweet and Sour Chicken Balls

75 g / 2 ½ oz / ½ cup plain
  (all-purpose) flour
75 g / 2 ½ oz / ½ cup cornflour
  (cornstarch)
1 tsp baking powder
1 tsp caster (superfine) sugar
1 tsp sesame oil
4 skinless chicken breasts, cut into
  bite-sized chunks
vegetable oil, for deep-frying

FOR THE SAUCE
125 ml / 4 ½ fl. oz / ½ cup pineapple juice
50 ml / 1 ¾ fl. oz / ¼ cup tomato ketchup
2 tbsp rice wine vinegar
2 tbsp light brown sugar
1 tsp soy sauce
1 tbsp cornflour (cornstarch)

1. To make the sauce, heat the pineapple juice, ketchup, vinegar, sugar and soy sauce
   together in a small saucepan. Slake the cornflour with 3 tablespoons of cold water,
   then stir it into the saucepan. Continue to stir over a medium heat until the sauce
   simmers and thickens. Transfer to serving pots and leave to cool.
2. Sieve the flour, cornflour, baking powder and sugar together. Stir the sesame oil
   into 150 ml of cold water, then whisk it into the flour to form a batter.
3. Heat the oil in a deep fat fryer, according to the manufacturer's instructions, to a
   temperature of 180°C (350F).
4. Dip the chicken breast chunks in batter and deep fry for 4 minutes or until
   nicely browned.
5. Drain the chicken on plenty of kitchen paper and serve with the sweet and sour
   sauce for dipping.

MAKES: 12 | PREP TIME: 2 HOURS 45 MINS | COOKING TIME: 12 MINS

Char Siu Buns

300 g / 10 ½ oz / 2 cups plain
   (all-purpose) flour
150 g / 5 ½ oz / 1 cup cornflour
   (cornstarch)
75 g / 2 ½ oz / ⅓ cup caster
   (superfine) sugar
1 tsp easy blend dried yeast
65 ml / 2 ¼ fl. oz / ⅓ cup vegetable oil
2 shallots, finely chopped
1 tbsp muscovado sugar
2 tbsp dark soy sauce
1 tbsp oyster sauce
1 tbsp sesame oil
100 ml / 3 ½ fl. oz / ½ cup chicken stock
225 g / 8 oz / 1 ½ cups Chinese roast
   pork, diced
2 ½ tsp baking powder
2 tbsp sesame seeds
1 red food colouring stamp (optional)

1. Reserve 1 tablespoons of flour and
   mix the rest with the cornflour, caster
   sugar and yeast. Stir 50 ml of oil into
   200 ml of warm water, then stir into
   the flour.

2. Knead the dough for 10 minutes, then
   cover and leave to rise for 2 hours.

3. Meanwhile, heat the remaining oil in a
   wok and fry the shallots for 2 minutes.
   Add the muscovado sugar, soy sauce,
   oyster sauce and sesame oil and bring
   to a simmer. Whisk in the reserved
   flour, then gradually incorporate the
   stock. When the mixture bubbles and
   thickens, stir in the diced pork and set
   aside to cool.

4. Knead the baking powder into the
   dough. Leave to rest for 15 minutes.

5. Divide the dough into twelve equal
   balls. Flatten each ball and add a
   spoonful of pork to the centre of each
   one. Gather up the edges and crimp
   to seal.

6. Sprinkle twelve squares of
   greaseproof paper with sesame seeds
   and place the buns on top, sealed
   side down. Steam the buns on the
   paper squares for 12 minutes,
   ensuring there's plenty of room for
   them to expand. Stamp the buns with
   red food colouring, if desired.

Spicy Chicken Noodle Soup

300 g / 10 ½ oz thin egg noodles
1 litre / 1 pint 14 fl. oz / 4 cups clear light
   chicken stock
2 tbsp shaoxing rice wine
1 tsp caster (superfine) sugar
1 red chilli (chili), sliced
1 green chilli (chili), sliced
2 skinless chicken breasts, cut into bite-
   sized chunks
1 handful coriander (cilantro) leaves

1. Cook the noodles in boiling water according to the packet instructions or until al dente. Plunge into cold water, then drain well.
2. Heat the stock in a saucepan with the rice wine, sugar and chillies. When it starts to boil, add the chicken and simmer very gently for 4 minutes or until just cooked through.
3. Add the noodles to the broth and warm through, then season to taste with salt.
4. Divide the soup between four bowls and serve garnished with coriander leaves.

Lemon Beef Stir Fry

2 tbsp vegetable oil
1 tbsp fresh root ginger, finely grated
1 sirloin steak, thinly sliced
2 sticks celery, sliced
4 spring onions, sliced
1 green pepper, cubed
1 red pepper, cubed
1 head broccoli, cut into florets
1 ½ lemons, juiced
2 tsp cornflour (cornstarch)
1 tbsp caster (superfine) sugar
2 tbsp light soy sauce

1. Heat the oil in a large wok and stir fry the ginger for 1 minute.
2. Add the steak and stir-fry for 3 minutes.
3. Add the vegetables and stir-fry over a high heat for 4 minutes.
4. Mix the lemon juice with the cornflour, sugar, soy sauce and 50 ml of water, then pour it into the wok and stir fry for 2 minutes. Serve immediately.

SERVES: 6 | PREP TIME: 15 MINS | MARINATING: 4 HOURS | COOKING: 6 MINS

Spare Ribs

1 ½ tbsp red fermented bean curd
2 tbsp shaoxing rice wine
1 tbsp light soy sauce
1 tbsp runny honey
1 tsp five spice powder
1 tsp garlic powder
½ tsp ground white pepper
900 g / 2 lb small ribs, separated
2 tbsp cornflour (cornstarch)
2 tbsp plain (all-purpose) flour
vegetable oil, for deep-frying
1 tbsp sesame seeds, toasted

1. Mash the bean curd into the rice wine, then whisk in the soy sauce, honey, five spice, garlic and white pepper. Add the ribs and toss well to coat. Leave to marinate in the fridge for 4 hours.

2. Heat the oil in a deep fat fryer, according to the manufacturer's instructions, to a temperature of 180°C (350F).

3. Sprinkle the cornflour and plain flour over the ribs and toss well to coat.

4. Deep fry the ribs in batches of six for 6 minutes or until deep golden brown and cooked through. Drain on plenty of kitchen paper.

5. Sprinkle the ribs with sesame seeds and serve immediately.

Crispy Sesame Chicken

vegetable oil, for deep frying
75 g / 2 ½ oz / ½ cup cornflour (cornstarch)
2 eggs, beaten
2 tsp sesame oil
100 g / 3 ½ oz / ⅔ cup panko breadcrumbs
30 g / 1 oz / ¼ cup sesame seeds
4 skinless chicken breasts, cut into strips

1. Heat the oil in a deep fat fryer, according to the manufacturer's instructions, to a temperature of 180°C (350F).
2. Put the cornflour in a bowl and season with salt and pepper. Beat the eggs with the sesame oil in a second bowl and mix the panko crumbs and sesame seeds in a third.
3. Dip the chicken strips first in the cornflour, then in the egg, then in the breadcrumbs.
4. Fry the chicken in batches for 5 minutes or until crisp and golden brown and then transfer to a drain on plenty of kitchen paper.
5. Serve immediately.

Mongolian Beef

2 tsp cornflour (cornstarch)
1 tbsp shaoxing rice wine
1 tbsp dark soy sauce
450 g / 1 lb / 3 cups fillet steak,
    thinly sliced
50 ml / 1 ¾ fl. oz / ¼ cup vegetable oil
3 clove of garlic, finely chopped
1 ½ tbsp fresh root ginger, finely julienned
6 spring onions (scallions), whites
    quartered lengthways, greens cut
    into short lengths
50 ml / 1 ¾ fl. oz / ¼ cup oyster sauce
2 tbsp runny honey
2 tbsp light soy sauce
½ tsp sesame oil
crispy rice noodles, to serve

1. Slake the cornflour with 2 tbsp of water, then stir in the rice wine and dark soy. Toss the steak with the mixture, then cover and marinate in the fridge for 1 hour.
2. Heat 2 tbsp of the oil in a large wok until smoking hot. Stir-fry the beef for 3 minutes or until sealed and lightly coloured. Transfer to a bowl and set aside, then clean the wok.
3. Heat the rest of the oil in the wok and fry the garlic and ginger for 1 minute. Add the spring onions and stir-fry for 2 minutes.
4. Return the beef to the wok, then add the oyster sauce, honey and light soy sauce. Stir-fry for 2 minutes, then stir in the sesame oil and taste the sauce for seasoning.
5. Serve immediately on a bed of crispy rice noodles.

SERVES: 4 | PREP TIME: 10 MINS | COOKING TIME: 10 MINS

Chicken Salad Open Wontons

12 wonton wrappers
2 tbsp vegetable oil
1 clove of garlic, crushed
2 tsp fresh root ginger, finely grated
3 skinless boneless chicken thighs, diced
1 tbsp oyster sauce
1 tsp sesame oil
½ red onion, finely diced
2 medium tomatoes, deseeded
  and finely diced

½ green pepper, deseeded and
  finely diced
1 lime, juiced
2 tbsp fresh coriander (cilantro) leaves,
  roughly chopped

1. Preheat the oven to 200°C (180°C fan) / 400F / gas 6. Brush the wonton wrappers with half of the oil, then drape them over the bars of a trivet set on a baking tray to make triangular pockets. Bake for 5 minutes or until crisp.
2. Heat the oil in a wok and fry the garlic and ginger for 1 minute. Add the chicken and stir-fry for 3 minutes, then stir in the oyster sauce and sesame oil and cook for 1 minute. Leave to cool.
3. Mix the chicken with the onion, tomatoes and peppers, then stir in the lime juice and coriander and taste with seasoning.
4. Fill the wonton pockets with the chicken mixture and serve immediately.

SERVES: **4** | PREP TIME: **3 HOURS 30 MINS** | COOKING TIME: **15 MINS**

Tea Eggs with Soba Noodles

4 large eggs
2 tbsp loose leaf tea
1 tbsp Chinese five spice powder
1 tbsp brown sugar
2 tbsp soy sauce
1 tsp sesame oil
400 g / 14 oz soba (buckwheat) noodles
2 tbsp vegetable oil
4 boneless chicken thighs, cubed, with skin left on
2 cloves of garlic, crushed
2 tsp fresh root ginger, finely grated
½ carrot, julienned
150 g / 5 ½ oz / 2 cups mushrooms, thickly sliced
75 ml / 2 ½ fl. oz / ⅓ cup oyster sauce
2 tbsp large peanuts

1. Boil the eggs for 8 minutes, then plunge into iced water and leave to cool for 5 minutes. Drain the eggs, then tap them all over with a teaspoon to crack the shell, being careful not to puncture the membrane underneath.

2. Measure the tea, spice powder, sugar and soy sauce into the saucepan. Add the eggs with enough cold water to just cover them. Cover and simmer very gently for 1 hour, then turn off the heat and leave to cool for 2 hours. Peel the eggs, rub with sesame oil and set aside.

3. Cook the noodles according to the packet instructions, then drain and plunge into iced water. Drain well.

4. Meanwhile, heat the oil in a large wok and fry the chicken skin side down for 4 minutes. Add the garlic and ginger and stir-fry for 2 minutes. Add the carrot and mushrooms and stir-fry for 4 minutes.

5. Add the oyster sauce, peanuts and 50 ml of water. When it starts to simmer, add the noodles and warm through.

6. Divide the noodles between four warm plates and top each one with a tea egg.

SERVES: 12 | **PREP TIME: 2 HOURS 45 MINS** | **COOKING TIME: 5 MINS**

Steamed Pork Belly Buns

450 g / 1 lb / 3 cups plain (all-purpose) flour
50 g / 1 ¾ oz / ¼ cup caster (superfine) sugar
2 tbsp dried skimmed milk powder
½ tsp easy blend dried yeast
450 g / 1 lb / 3 cups pork belly, cubed
2 tbsp vegetable oil
1 tbsp runny honey
3 tbsp shaoxing rice wine
1 tbsp light soy sauce
½ tbsp dark soy sauce
2 tbsp sesame oil
shredded mooli (daikon), to serve
chopped spring onions (scallions) and coriander (cilantro), to garnish

1. Mix the flour with the sugar, milk powder and yeast. Stir in enough warm water to form a soft dough (around 250 ml).

2. Knead the dough for 10 minutes, then cover and leave to rise for 2 hours.

3. Meanwhile, blanch the pork for 2 minutes in boiling water. Drain and dry with kitchen paper.

4. Heat the oil in a wok, add the pork and stir-fry for 4 minutes. Drizzle with honey and stir-fry until browned. Add the rice wine, soy sauces and 500 ml of water, then simmer gently for 1 hour, stirring occasionally. Increase the heat and boil until reduced to a thick sauce. Keep warm.

5. When the dough has risen, knead in the baking powder and leave to rest for 15 minutes.

6. Divide the dough into twelve equal balls. Flatten each ball, brush with sesame oil and fold in half. Leave each one to rise on a square of oiled greaseproof paper for 30 minutes.

7. Steam the buns on the paper squares for 5 minutes, leaving plenty of room to expand. Unfold the buns and fill with shredded mooli and pork belly, then garnish with spring onion and coriander.

MAKES: 40 | PREP TIME: 4 HOURS | CHILL: OVERNIGHT | COOKING: 8 MINS

Shanghai Soup Dumplings

1 chicken carcass, broken into pieces
1 small ham hock
2 tbsp fresh root ginger, sliced
1 tbsp white peppercorns
6 spring onions (scallions), finely chopped
300 g / 10 ½ oz / 2 cups plain (all-purpose) flour
150 g / 5 ½ oz / 1 cup minced pork
150 g / 5 ½ oz / 1 cup raw prawns (shrimp), finely chopped
1 tbsp shaoxing rice wine
1 tbsp light soy sauce
2 tsp caster (superfine) sugar
coriander (cilantro) leaves, to garnish

1. Put the chicken carcass and ham hock in a large saucepan with the ginger, peppercorns and two thirds of the spring onions. Add enough cold water to just cover the ingredients, then bring to the boil. Reduce the heat and simmer for 3 hours, then strain into a plastic container. Leave to cool, then refrigerate overnight.
2. Sift the flour into a bowl and stir in 250 ml of recently boiled water. Knead for 8 minutes or until smooth, adding more flour if necessary. Rest for 30 minutes.
3. Meanwhile, put the pork, prawns, rice wine, soy sauce, sugar, and the rest of the spring onions in a food processor and pulse to a paste. Add 250 ml of the jellied stock and blend again, then chill until ready to use.
4. Divide the rested dough into 40 balls, then flatten them. Add 1 tablespoon of filling to each wrapper, pleating round the outside and pinching to seal in the centre.
5. Space out the siu mai in oiled steamer baskets and steam for 8 minutes.
6. Serve immediately, garnished with coriander, being careful not to pierce them.

MAKES: 24 | PREP TIME: 20 MINS | COOKING TIME: 12 MINS

Pork and Prawn Siu Mai

350 g / 12 ½ oz / 2 ⅓ cups minced pork
175 g / 6 oz / 1 ¼ cups raw prawns
  (shrimp), finely chopped
50 g / 1 ¾ oz / ½ cup canned water
  chestnuts, finely chopped
2 spring onions (scallions),
  finely chopped
1 tsp fresh root ginger, finely grated
1 ½ tbsp shaoxing rice wine
2 tbsp light soy sauce
2 tsp sesame oil
1 ½ tbsp cornflour (cornstarch)
24 round egg wonton wrappers
1 egg white, beaten
24 salmon eggs

1. Mix the pork with the prawns, water chestnuts, spring onions, ginger, rice wine, soy sauce, sesame oil and cornflour. Season with 1 teaspoon of salt and some freshly ground white pepper.
2. Put a tablespoon of filling in the centre of each wonton wrapper, then brush round the edge with egg white. Gather up the edges and squeeze gently to seal, then top each one with a single salmon egg.
3. Space out the siu mai in oiled steamer baskets and steam for 12 minutes, then serve immediately.

Quinoa and Chinese Sausage Spring Rolls

150 g / 5 ½ oz / ¾ cup quinoa
1 tbsp vegetable oil
1 clove of garlic, crushed
1 tsp fresh root ginger, finely grated
1 Chinese sausage, diced
1 small courgette (zucchini), diced
½ yellow pepper, finely chopped
6 rice paper wrappers
vegetable oil, for deep frying
coriander (cilantro), to garnish

1. Put the quinoa in a saucepan with 150 ml water. Cover and simmer gently for 10 minutes, then leave to stand off the heat for a further 15 minutes without lifting the lid.
2. Heat 1 tablespoon of vegetable oil in a wok and stir-fry the garlic and ginger for 30 seconds. Add the sausage, zucchini and pepper and stir-fry for 3 minutes. Take the pan off the heat and stir in the quinoa.
3. Dip the first rice paper wrapper in a bowl of cold water, then lay it out on a clean chopping board. Spoon a sixth of the filling on top. Fold over the sides of the wrapper, then roll it up to enclose the filling. Repeat with the rest to form six rolls.
4. Heat the oil in a deep fat fryer, according to the manufacturer's instructions, to a temperature of 180°C (350 F).
5. Deep fry the spring rolls in two batches for 5 minutes or until lightly golden and very crisp.
6. Drain on plenty of kitchen paper and serve, garnished with chopped coriander.

Beef with Peppers and Beans

2 tbsp vegetable oil
3 cloves of garlic, finely chopped
1 tbsp fresh root ginger, finely chopped
4 spring onions (scallions), sliced
    diagonally, white and green
    parts separated
2 sirloin steaks, thinly sliced
150 g / 5 ½ oz / 1 cup green beans,
    cut into short lengths
1 yellow pepper, quartered and sliced
50 ml / 1 ¾ fl. oz / ¼ cup shaoxing rice wine
75 ml / 2 ½ fl. oz / ⅓ cup oyster sauce

1. Heat the oil in a large wok and stir fry the ginger, garlic and spring onion whites for 1 minute. Add the steak and stir-fry for 3 minutes.
2. Add the vegetables and stir-fry for 2 minutes. Add the rice wine and 50 ml of water, then cover the wok with a lid and steam for 2 minutes.
3. Stir in the oyster sauce and stir-fry for 2 minutes, then serve garnished with spring onion greens.

SERVES: **4** | PREP TIME: **10 MINS** | COOKING TIME: **10 MINS**

Chicken Noodle Stir Fry

200 g / 7 oz wide flat rice noodles
2 tbsp vegetable oil
2 cloves of garlic, thinly sliced
1 tbsp fresh root ginger, thinly sliced
4 spring onions (scallions), whites chopped, greens cut into short lengths
2 skinless chicken breasts, sliced
1 large carrot, julienned with a mandolin
¼ Chinese cabbage, thinly sliced
2 tbsp light soy sauce

1. Cook the noodles in boiling water according to the packet instructions or until al dente, then drain well.
2. Heat the oil in a large wok and fry the garlic, ginger and spring onion whites for 2 minutes.
3. Add the chicken and stir fry for 3 minutes or until lightly coloured. Add the carrots and cabbage and stir-fry for 2 minutes.
4. Add the soy sauce, noodles and spring onion greens and stir-fry for 2 more minutes, then taste and adjust the seasoning with a little more soy sauce if needed.
5. Serve immediately.

Grilled Chicken with Noodles

2 large skinless chicken breasts
2 tbsp light soy sauce
1 tbsp runny honey
1 tsp five spice powder
1 lime, juiced
400 g / 14 oz thin egg noodles
2 tbsp sunflower oil
2 cloves of garlic, sliced
2 tsp fresh root ginger, finely chopped
4 spring onions (scallions), chopped, green and white parts separated
2 mild red chillies (chilies), sliced
1 carrot, julienned
1 tsp sesame oil
coriander (cilantro) leaves, to garnish

1. Put the chicken in a freezer bag with the soy, honey, spices and lime juice. Massage to coat, then marinate in the fridge for 1 hour. Cook the noodles according to packet instructions, then drain and plunge into iced water. Drain well.
2. Cook the chicken under a hot grill for 4 minutes on each side, or until only just cooked in the centre. Meanwhile, heat the oil in a large wok and fry the garlic, ginger, spring onion whites and chillies for 2 minutes.
3. Add the carrot and stir-fry for 2 minutes, then pour in the marinade from the freezer bag. As soon as it starts to bubble, add the noodles and sesame oil and heat through. Divide the noodles between four warm bowls and garnish with spring onion greens and coriander.
4. Slice the chicken and divide between the bowls. Serve immediately.

Chicken and Noodles with Oyster Sauce

300 g / 10 ½ oz wide wheat noodles
2 tbsp vegetable oil
2 cloves of garlic, thinly sliced
1 tbsp root ginger, thinly sliced
300 g / 10 ½ oz / 2 cups skinless boneless chicken thighs, sliced
1 large carrot, julienned
2 large mild red chillies (chilies), sliced diagonally
2 tbsp shaoxing rice wine
50 ml / 1 ¾ fl. oz / ¼ cup oyster sauce
2 tsp sesame oil
1 handful fresh coriander (cilantro), chopped

1. Cook the noodles in boiling water according to the packet instructions or until al dente, then drain well.
2. Heat the oil in a large wok and fry the garlic and ginger for 2 minutes.
3. Add the chicken and stir fry for 3 minutes or until lightly coloured. Add the carrots and chillies and stir-fry for 2 minutes.
4. Add the rice wine, oyster sauce and sesame oil and stir well. Add the noodles and stir-fry for 2 more minutes. Serve immediately, garnished with coriander.

SERVES: 6 | PREP TIME: 20 MINS | MARINATE: OVERNIGHT | COOK: 1 HR 45 MINS

Roast Pork Belly Noodles

1.5 kg / 3 lb 12 ½ oz boneless pork belly, skin pricked all over
50 ml / 1 ¾ fl. oz / ¼ cup light soy sauce
2 tsp five spice powder
400 g / 14 oz thin egg noodles
1 tbsp vegetable oil
1 tbsp fresh root ginger, sliced
2 cloves of garlic, sliced
1.2 litres / 2 pints / 4 ¾ cups pork or chicken stock
1 orange pepper, quartered, deseeded and sliced
2 pak choi, leaves separated
6 poached eggs, to serve
2 large salad onions, whites sliced into rings, greens chopped
soy sauce with chilli, for dipping

1. Put the pork belly on a trivet in the sink, skin side up, and pour over a kettle of boiling water.
2. Dry thoroughly with kitchen paper, then rub 1 teaspoon of salt into the skin.
3. Mix the soy sauce and five spice in a wide bowl, then add the pork, flesh side down. Marinate, uncovered, in the fridge overnight.
4. Preheat the oven to its highest temperature. Transfer the pork to a roasting tin and dry the skin thoroughly. Roast for 30 minutes.
5. Reduce the temperature to 160°C (140°C fan) / 325F / gas 3 and roast for 1 hour.
6. Cook the noodles in boiling water according to the packet instructions, then drain well and divide between six warm bowls.
7. Heat the oil in a large wok and fry the ginger and garlic for 2 minutes. Add the stock and bring to the boil. Add the pepper and pak choi and simmer for 2 minutes.
8. Remove the crackling from the pork and break into chunks. Cut the pork into bite-sized pieces. Divide the pak choi, peppers and poached eggs between the bowls and ladle over the broth. Top with pork, crackling and salad onions.

Chicken and Coconut Soup

1 kg whole small chicken
50 g / 1 ¾ oz / ⅓ cup fresh root ginger, sliced
5 cloves of garlic, squashed
6 spring onions (scallions), tied into a knot
2 leeks, sliced
800 ml / 1 pint 7 fl. oz / 3 ¼ cups canned
   coconut milk
1 small bunch fresh coriander
   (cilantro), chopped
½ tbsp caster (superfine) sugar
2 tbsp light soy sauce
1 lime, juiced

1. Rub the chicken inside and out with 2 tsp of salt, then stuff the cavity with ginger, garlic and spring onions. Have a kettle of boiling water at the ready.
2. Put the leeks and coconut milk in a saucepan large enough to accommodate the chicken and bring to the boil. Carefully lower in the chicken, then add enough boiling water to cover the chicken by 2.5 cm (1 in).
3. When the liquid returns to the boil, lower the heat and simmer gently for 15 minutes. Turn off the hob, cover the pan and leave the chicken to cook in the residual heat for 30 minutes.
4. Carefully remove the chicken from the put and discard the skin. Pull the meat off the carcass and cut it into bite-sized pieces, then return it to the saucepan.
5. Bring the soup to a gentle simmer and stir in half of the coriander. Season to taste with sugar, soy sauce and lime juice.
6. Ladle the soup into bowls and garnish with black pepper and extra coriander.

Chicken and Snake Beans

2 tbsp vegetable oil
1 red onion, sliced
2 cloves of garlic, thinly sliced
1 tbsp root ginger, thinly sliced
2 skinless chicken breasts, sliced
6 young snake beans, halved if very long
2 tbsp light soy sauce
1 small carrot, spiralised or julienned
50 g / 1 ¾ oz / 1 cup beansprouts

1. Heat the oil in a large wok and fry the onion, garlic and ginger for 2 minutes.
2. Add the chicken and stir fry for 3 minutes or until lightly coloured. Add the snake beans and stir-fry for 1 minute.
3. Add the soy sauce and 40 ml of water, then cover and steam for 4 minutes.
4. Add the carrot and beansprouts and stir-fry for 2 minutes, then serve immediately.

Braised Beef with Noodles

600 g / 1 lb 5 ½ oz / 4 cups braising steak,
  cut into bite-sized chunks
1 tsp five spice powder
2 tbsp vegetable oil
1 tbsp runny honey
3 tbsp shaoxing rice wine
1 tbsp light soy sauce
½ tbsp dark soy sauce
1 tbsp sesame oil
400 g / 14 oz medium egg noodles
coriander (cilantro), to garnish

1. Dry the beef thoroughly with kitchen paper, then season with salt and five spice.
2. Heat the oil in a wok, add the beef and stir-fry for 4 minutes. Drizzle with honey and stir-fry until browned. Add the rice wine, soy sauces and 500 ml of water.
3. Cover and simmer gently for 2 hours or until tender, stirring occasionally. Cook the noodles according to the packet instructions or until al dente, then drain well.
4. Stir the noodles into the beef pan, then divide between four warm bowls and serve immediately, garnished with coriander.

Char Siu Pork Noodle Soup

2 tbsp hoisin sauce
2 tbsp sweet soy sauce or kecap manis
2 tbsp runny honey
1 tsp five spice powder
1 tbsp vegetable oil
1 tsp sesame oil
a few drops red food colouring
450 g / 1 lb whole pork tenderloin
1.2 litres / 2 pints / 4 ¾ cups pork or
  chicken stock
400 g / 14 oz thin egg noodles
4 slices leftover roast pork belly, cut into
  bite-sized pieces
4 spring onions (scallions), sliced, green
  parts only
1 small bunch fresh coriander
  (cilantro), chopped

1. Put the hoisin, soy, honey, five spice, vegetable oil, sesame oil and food colouring in a saucepan. Stir continuously while it comes to the boil, then leave to cool. Scrape the mixture into a freezer bag, add the pork and massage well to coat. Marinate in the fridge overnight.
2. Preheat the oven to 180°C (160°C fan) / 350F / gas 4 and line a roasting tin with greaseproof paper. Transfer the pork to the tin and roast for 25 minutes, basting with marinade twice, part way through.
3. Meanwhile, heat the stock in a saucepan. Cook the noodles in boiling water according to packet instructions, then drain and divide between six warm bowls. Slice the pork tenderloin and divide between the bowls and add some pork belly and spring onion greens to each one.
4. Ladle over the stock, sprinkle with coriander and serve immediately.

SERVES: 6 | **PREP TIME: 15 MINS** | **COOKING TIME: 1 HOUR 10 MINS**

Braised Duck with Noodles

1.8 kg / 4 lb whole duck
75 ml / 2 ½ fl. oz / ⅓ cup dark soy sauce
2 tbsp shaoxing rice wine
1 tsp caster (superfine) sugar
2 stalks lemongrass, bruised
4 slices fresh root ginger
4 spring onions (scallions), chopped, green and white parts separated
2 star anise
2 cloves of garlic, squashed
400 g / 14 oz vermicelli rice noodles
150 g / 5 ½ oz / 4 ½ cups ong choi (water spinach)

1. Rub the duck inside and out with 1 tbsp of salt. Put the soy sauce, rice wine, sugar, lemongrass, ginger, spring onion whites, star anise and garlic in a saucepan large enough to accommodate the duck. Stir in 750 ml of water.
2. Bring to the boil, then carefully lower in the duck, breast side down. Cover and simmer gently for 30 minutes, adding a little boiling water if the liquid level falls below halfway up the duck.
3. Turn the duck over, then cover and simmer for 30 minutes or until the meat pulls easily away from the bones.
4. Cook the noodles in boiling water according to the packet instructions or until al dente. Drain well and divide between six bowls.
5. Carefully transfer the duck to a carving board and scoop out and discard the flavourings from the broth. Add the ong choi to the broth and simmer for 5 minutes while you carve the duck.
6. Divide the duck and ong choi between the bowls. Taste the broth and either season with salt or dilute with a little water if too strong. Ladle a little into each bowl and serve, garnished with spring onion greens.

MAKES: 16 | **PREP TIME: 30 MINS** | **RESTING: 1 HOUR** | **COOKING TIME: 3 MINS**

Duck Pancakes

350 g / 12 ½ z / 1 ½ cups plain
  (all-purpose) flour
1 tsp sesame oil

TO SERVE
100 ml / 3 ½ fl. oz / ½ cup hoisin sauce
½ Cantonese roast duck, boned
  and sliced
1 small cucumber, julienned
3 spring onions (scallions), julienned

1. Mix the flour with ½ teaspoon of salt
   in a bowl. Stir in 150 ml boiling water,
   adding a little more if needed to form
   a soft dough. When it has cooled
   down enough to handle, knead for
   5 minutes, then cover and leave to
   rest for 1 hour.

2. Divide the dough into sixteen balls
   and flatten them slightly. Brush the
   top of the discs with sesame oil and
   sandwich them together with the
   oiled sides touching. Roll out the
   discs on a lightly floured surface into
   7.5 cm (3 in) circles.

3. Heat a frying pan over a medium heat
   without any oil. Fry one of the
   pancakes for 30 seconds or until it
   starts to puff slightly. Flip it over and
   cook the other side until lightly
   coloured in places. Peel the pancake
   apart and transfer to a covered
   steamer basket. Repeat with the rest
   of the pancakes.

4. When you're ready to serve, steam
   the pancakes for 2 minutes.

5. Take them to the table with the
   accompaniments and encourage each
   person to top a pancake with a smear
   of hoisin, a few slices of duck and
   some cucumber and spring onion.

SERVES: **4** | PREP TIME: **5 MINS** | COOKING TIME: **10 MINS**

Chicken and Egg Noodle Soup

400 g / 14 oz medium egg noodles
1 tbsp rice wine vinegar
4 very fresh eggs
1.2 litres / 2 pints / 4 ¾ cups pork or chicken stock
1 large chicken breast, sliced
12 baby sweetcorn, cut into bite-sized chunks
100 g / 3 ½ oz / 1 ½ cups oyster mushrooms, torn into bite-sized chunks if large
¼ Chinese cabbage, shredded
1 handful beansprouts
2 spring onions (scallions), chopped, green parts only
1 tbsp chilli paste

1. Cook the noodles in boiling water according to the packet instructions, then drain and divide between four warm bowls.
2. At the same time, bring a saucepan of water to a gentle simmer and stir in the vinegar. Crack each egg into a cup then pour them smoothly into the water, one at a time. Poach gently for 3 minutes. Remove the eggs from the pan with a slotted spoon and transfer to a bowl of cold water.
3. Meanwhile, bring the stock to the boil in a separate saucepan. Add the chicken and sweetcorn and poach gently for 3 minutes. Add the mushrooms and cabbage and poach for 2 minutes. Add the beansprouts and poach for 1 minute.
4. Divide the soup between the bowls and top each one with a poached egg, a sprinkle of spring onion greens and a little chilli paste.

Chicken and Shiitake Congee

30 g / 1 oz / ½ cup dried shiitake mushrooms
700 g / 1 lb 9 oz / 5 cups skinless chicken
  thighs, on the bone
4 spring onions (scallions), chopped, green
  and white parts separated
5 cm (2 in) fresh root ginger, half thickly
  sliced, half finely julienned
200 g / 7 oz / 1 cup long grain rice
1 litre / 17 ½ fl. oz / 4 cups chicken stock
100 g / 3 ½ oz / ½ cup canned bamboo
  shoots, finely julienned

1. Soak the shiitakes in boiling water for 20 minutes, then drain and thinly slice.
2. Put the shiitakes in a large saucepan with the chicken, spring onion whites, sliced ginger and rice. Cover with the chicken stock and 1.5 litres of water, then stir in 2 teaspoons of salt.
3. Bring the mixture to the boil, then reduce the heat and simmer for 1 hour or until the rice has broken down into a thick porridge, stirring occasionally.
4. Transfer the chicken to a chopping board, remove the bones and slice it thickly. Stir the chicken back into the pot, then taste and adjust the seasoning with salt and white pepper. Ladle the congee into six bowls and top with julienned ginger, bamboo shoots and spring onion greens.

Braised Brisket Noodle Soup

1 tbsp vegetable oil
600 g / 1 lb 5 ½ oz beef brisket, in one piece
4 large shallots, unpeeled
25 g / 1 oz fresh root ginger, in one piece
1 carrot, cut into large chunks
8 cloves
1 tbsp white peppercorns
2 star anise
1 tbsp caster (superfine) sugar
50 ml / 1 ¾ fl. oz / ¼ cup fish sauce
300 g / 10 ½ oz glass noodles
150 g / 5 ½ oz / 1 ½ cup shimeji mushrooms
4 baby pak choi, leaves separated
1 red chilli (chili), sliced

1. Heat the vegetable oil in a frying pan and sear the beef until browned. Meanwhile, toast the shallots, ginger and carrot under a hot grill until dark brown all over.
2. Transfer the beef and toasted vegetables to a large saucepan and add the cloves, peppercorns, star anise, sugar and fish sauce. Pour over 1.5 litres of water.
3. Bring to the boil, then cover and simmer gently for 3 hours or until the beef is tender. Transfer the beef to a carving board and cover with a double layer of foil, then strain the stock to get rid of the vegetables and spices. Return the stock to the pan.
4. Prepare the glass noodles according to the packet instructions and divide between four bowls. Cook the mushrooms and pak choi in the beef stock for 3 minutes or until tender, while you slice the beef.
5. Divide the beef, pak choi and mushrooms between the bowls and ladle some stock over each. Garnish with chillies and serve immediately.

SERVES: **4** | PREP TIME: **35 MINS** | COOKING TIME: **8 MINS**

Chicken and Mushroom Wui Fan

3 skinless chicken breasts, cut into
   bite-sized chunks
150 g / 5 ½ oz / 1 ½ cup king oyster
   mushrooms, chopped if large
2 tbsp light soy sauce
2 tsp sesame oil
2 tsp cornflour (cornstarch)
½ tsp ground white pepper
2 tbsp vegetable oil
2 cloves of garlic, finely chopped
½ tbsp root ginger, finely chopped
4 spring onions (scallions), chopped,
   green and white parts separated
250 ml / 9 fl. oz / 1 cup chicken stock
2 tbsp oyster sauce
1 medium egg, beaten
450 g / 1 lb / 2 ½ cups freshly cooked
   long grain rice
1 handful fresh coriander (cilantro) leaves

1. Marinate the chicken and mushrooms in half the soy sauce, half the sesame oil, half the cornflour and the white pepper for 30 minutes.

2. Heat the vegetable oil in a wok and fry the garlic, ginger and spring onion whites for 1 minute. Add the chicken and mushrooms and stir-fry for 2 minutes. Add the stock and oyster sauce and bring to a simmer. Cook for 2 minutes.

3. Move the chicken and mushrooms to the side of the wok. Slake the cornflour with the rest of the soy sauce and whisk it into the sauce. When it thickens, whisk in the egg, then fold in the rice.

4. Divide the mixture between four bowls and top with spring onion greens and coriander leaves.

Beef and Rice Noodle Soup

4 large shallots, unpeeled
8 cloves
25 g / 1 oz fresh root ginger, in one piece
2 parsnips, cut into large chunks
900 g / 2 lb meaty beef bones (e.g. oxtail)
1 tbsp white peppercorns
2 star anise
1 tbsp caster (superfine) sugar
50 ml / 1 ¾ fl. oz / ¼ cup fish sauce
300 g / 10 ½ oz flat rice noodles
1 small fillet steak, very thinly sliced
1 handful beansprouts
2 chillies (chilies), sliced
½ red onion, thinly sliced
1 handful fresh coriander (cilantro) leaves

1. Stud the shallots with cloves, then toast them under a hot grill with the ginger and parsnips until brown all over.
2. Transfer the vegetables to a large saucepan and add the bones, peppercorns, star anise, sugar and fish sauce. Pour over 1.5 litres of water.
3. Bring to the boil, then cover and simmer gently for 2 hours. Strain the broth to get rid of the bones and vegetables, then return it to the pan and bring to a simmer.
4. Prepare the noodles according to the packet instructions and divide between four bowls. Top with the raw steak, beansprouts, chillies and onion, then ladle over the hot broth. Garnish with coriander leaves and serve immediately.

Fried Chicken Wing Drumettes

vegetable oil, for deep frying
75 g / 2 ½ oz / ½ cup plain (all-purpose) flour
½ tsp five spice powder
1 large egg, separated
150 ml / 5 ½ fl. oz / ⅔ cup sparkling water
2 tbsp black sesame seeds
12 large chicken wing drumettes

1. Heat the oil in a deep fat fryer, according to the manufacturer's instructions, to a temperature of 180°C (350F).
2. Mix 60 g of flour with the five spice and ½ a teaspoon of salt and make a well in the middle. Add the egg yolk and sparkling water, then whisk them together, gradually incorporating all the flour from round the outside. Whip the egg white until stiff, then fold it into the batter with the sesame seeds.
3. Toss the chicken with the rest of the flour and shake off any excess. Working in batches, dip the chicken in the batter, then deep-fry for 6 minutes or until brown and cooked through.
4. Drain on kitchen paper and serve immediately.

SERVES: 4 | PREP TIME: 20 MINS | COOKING TIME: 6 MINS

Breaded Chicken with Pineapple

1 tbsp vegetable oil, plus extra for deep-frying
1 red chilli (chili), chopped
2 cloves of garlic, finely chopped
2 tsp fresh root ginger, finely chopped
225 g / 8 oz / 1 small can pineapple chunks in juice
2 tbsp rice wine vinegar
2 tbsp light brown sugar
1 tbsp soy sauce
1 tsp cornflour (cornstarch)
75 g / 2 ½ oz / ½ cup plain (all-purpose) flour
2 eggs, beaten
100 g / 3 ½ oz / 1 cup panko breadcrumbs
4 small skinless chicken breasts
steamed rice, to serve
2 tbsp fresh coriander (cilantro), chopped

1. Heat 1 tbsp vegetable oil in a wok and fry the chilli, garlic and ginger for 1 minute.
   Add the pineapple chunks and their juice, plus the vinegar, sugar and soy sauce.
2. When the sauce starts to simmer, slake the cornflour with 2 tablespoons of cold
   water, then stir it into the wok. Continue to stir over a medium heat until the sauce
   simmers and thickens.
3. Heat the oil in a deep fat fryer, according to the manufacturer's instructions, to a
   temperature of 180°C (350F).
4. Put the flour, egg and breadcrumbs in three separate bowls and dip the chicken
   breasts alternately in each one. Deep-fry the chicken in two batches for 6 minutes
   or until nicely browned and cooked through.
5. Drain the chicken on plenty of kitchen paper and serve on a bed of rice with the
   pineapple sauce spooned over. Garnish with coriander.

Lion's Head Meatballs

450 g / 1 lb / 3 cups minced pork
150 g / 5 ½ oz / 1 cup water chestnuts,
   finely chopped
1 tsp fresh root ginger, finely grated
4 spring onions (scallions), whites finely
   chopped, greens sliced
50 ml / 1 ¾ fl. oz / ¼ cup shaoxing rice wine
2 tbsp light soy sauce
1 tbsp dark soy sauce
1 tbsp sesame oil
1 tbsp caster (superfine) sugar
3 medium eggs, beaten
1 tbsp cornflour (cornstarch)
100 g / 3 ½ oz / 1 cup panko breadcrumbs
2 tbsp vegetable oil
1 tbsp sesame seeds

1. Put the pork in a large mixing bowl and beat in 60 ml of cold water. Add the water chestnuts, ginger and spring onion whites and mix well.

2. Whisk the rice wine with the soy sauces, sesame oil, sugar and eggs, then slowly incorporate it into the pork mixture. Mix the cornflour with the breadcrumbs, then work it into the pork.

3. Shape the mixture into 16 meatballs, then cover and chill in the fridge for 30 minutes. Heat the vegetable oil in a large frying pan and sear the meatballs until browned all over. Transfer the meatballs to a plate set in a steamer and steam for 15 minutes or until cooked through.

4. Skewer each meatball onto a wooden cocktail fork and transfer to a serving plate. Drizzle over the cooking juices and sprinkle with sesame seeds and spring onion greens before serving.

Beef, Egg and Choi Sum with Rice

2 tbsp vegetable oil
1 clove of garlic, crushed
1 tsp fresh root ginger, finely grated
1 small sirloin steak, very thinly sliced
1 tbsp shaoxing rice wine
1 tbsp oyster sauce
30 g / 1 oz / 1 cup choi sum, cut into
   short lengths
2 medium eggs
½ tsp light soy sauce
steamed rice, to serve

1. Heat 1 tablespoon of the oil in a wok and fry the garlic and ginger for 1 minute. Add the steak and stir-fry for 2 minutes. Add the rice wine and oyster sauce and stir-fry for 1 minute. Cover and set aside.

2. Meanwhile, steam the choi sum for 2 minutes or until just tender.

3. Heat the rest of the oil in a frying pan. Beat the eggs with the soy sauce, then pour it into the pan and swirl to coat the bottom. Cook until just set, then turn the omelette out onto a chopping board and slice it into ribbons.

4. Serve the beef, omelette and choi sum on a bed of steamed rice.

Cantonese Roast Duck

1.8 kg / 4 lb whole duck
1 tbsp vegetable oil
75 ml / 2 ½ fl. oz / ⅓ cup dark soy sauce
100 ml / 3 ½ fl. oz / ½ cup shaoxing
   rice wine
1 tbsp demerara sugar
2 tbsp rice wine vinegar
4 cloves of garlic, squashed
4 slices fresh root ginger
4 spring onions (scallions), tied in a knot
2 star anise
4 pieces dried orange peel
6 cloves
1 tbsp white peppercorns
2 tbsp runny honey

1. Rub the duck inside and out with
   1 tbsp of salt. Heat the oil in a large
   wok and swirl to coat, then sear the
   duck all over until nicely browned.

2. Put the soy sauce, rice wine, sugar,
   vinegar, garlic, ginger, spring onion
   whites, star anise, cloves and
   peppercorns in a saucepan large
   enough to accommodate the duck.
   Stir in 750 ml of water.

3. Bring to the boil, then carefully lower
   in the duck, breast side down.
   Cover and simmer gently for 1 hour,
   turning the duck every 15 minutes.

4. Preheat the oven to 220°C (200°C fan)
   / 425F / gas 7. Transfer the duck to a
   trivet inside a large roasting tin.
   Dry the skin well with kitchen paper.

5. Roast the duck for 10 minutes.
   Brush the duck all over with honey,
   then return to the oven for 10 minutes
   or until the skin is nicely lacquered.

6. Leave the duck to rest for 15 minutes,
   then remove the meat from the bones
   and cut into slices.

Chicken and Vegetable Fried Rice

2 tbsp vegetable oil
1 small onion, sliced
2 cloves of garlic, thinly sliced
1 tbsp root ginger, thinly sliced
1 orange pepper, deseeded, quartered
  and sliced
1 head broccoli, cut into florets
1 courgette (zucchini), thinly sliced
50 ml / 1 ¾ fl. oz / ¼ cup shaoxing rice wine
2 cold roast chicken breasts, skinned and
  turn into chunks
75 g / 2 ½ oz / ½ cup frozen peas, defrosted
500 g / 17 ½ oz / 3 cups long grain rice,
  cooked and cooled
2 tbsp light soy sauce
2 tsp sesame oil

1. Heat the vegetable oil in a large wok and fry the onion, garlic and ginger for
   1 minute.
2. Add the vegetables and fry for 4 minutes. Pour over the rice wine, then cover and
   steam for 2 minutes.
3. Add the chicken, peas and rice and stir fry until piping hot – this should take about
   4 minutes. Season the rice with soy sauce and sesame oil, then divide between
   four plates and serve immediately.

Turkey Noodle Soup

4 large eggs
300 g / 10 ½ oz thin egg noodles
1 litre / 1 pint 14 fl. oz / 4 cups chicken stock
2 tbsp shaoxing rice wine
1 tsp caster (superfine) sugar
2 tbsp dark soy sauce
2 turkey breast fillets
3 spring onions (scallions), chopped,
  green parts only
2 tsp chilli (chili) flakes

1. Put the eggs in a saucepan of cold water and bring to the boil. Reduce the heat and
   simmer gently for 5 minutes, then plunge into iced water. Wait for 5 minutes, then
   peel and halve the eggs.
2. Meanwhile, cook the noodles in boiling water according to the packet instructions
   or until al dente. Divide between four bowls.
3. Heat the stock in a saucepan with the rice wine, sugar and soy sauce. When it starts
   to boil, add the turkey and poach very gently for 6 minutes or until just cooked
   through. Remove the turkey from the broth and cut it into slices, then arrange on
   top of the noodles.
4. Season the broth to taste, then ladle it over the noodles and garnish with the eggs,
   spring onion greens and chilli flakes.

SERVES: 4 | PREP TIME: 10 MINS | MARINATE: 3 HOURS | COOKING: 15 MINS

Satay Beef Noodle Soup

75 g / 2 ½ oz / ⅓ cup smooth peanut butter
1 tbsp runny honey
2 tbsp dark soy sauce
1 tsp five spice powder
1 clove of garlic, crushed
300 g / 10 ½ oz / 2 cups rump steak, very thinly sliced
300 g / 10 ½ oz thin rice noodles
2 tbsp vegetable oil
2 red chillies (chilies), chopped
2 tsp fresh root ginger, finely chopped
½ green pepper, diced
150 g / 5 ½ oz / 1 cup canned pineapple, drained and diced
1 litre / 1 pint 14 fl. oz / 4 cups beef stock

1. Mix the peanut butter with the honey, soy sauce, five spice and garlic. Add the steak and stir well to coat, then marinate in the fridge for 3 hours.
2. Cook the noodles in boiling water according to the packet instructions or until al dente. Drain well and divide between four bowls.
3. Heat the oil in a wok and stir-fry the chillies and ginger for 1 minute. Add the green pepper and stir-fry for 2 minutes.
4. Add the beef and marinade and stir-fry for 3 minutes or until just cooked. Add the pineapple and stock and bring to a simmer, then ladle over the noodles and serve immediately.

SERVES: 4 | PREP TIME: **10 MINS** | MARINATE: **3 HOURS** | COOKING: **15 MINS**

Steak and Peanut Noodles

75 g / 2 ½ oz / ⅓ cup smooth peanut butter
1 tbsp runny honey
2 tbsp dark soy sauce
1 tsp five spice powder
1 clove of garlic, crushed
300 g / 10 ½ oz / 2 cups rump steak, very thinly sliced
300 g / 10 ½ oz thin rice noodles
2 tbsp vegetable oil
2 red chillies (chilies), chopped
2 tsp fresh root ginger, finely chopped
½ green pepper, diced
150 g / 5 ½ oz / 1 cup canned pineapple, drained and diced
1 litre / 1 pint 14 fl. oz / 4 cups beef stock

1. Mix the peanut butter with the honey, soy sauce, five spice and garlic. Add the steak and stir well to coat, then marinate in the fridge for 3 hours.
2. Cook the noodles in boiling water according to the packet instructions or until al dente. Drain well and divide between four bowls.
3. Heat the oil in a wok and stir-fry the chillies and ginger for 1 minute. Add the green pepper and stir-fry for 2 minutes.
4. Add the beef and marinade and stir-fry for 3 minutes or until just cooked. Add the pineapple and stock and bring to a simmer, then ladle over the noodles and serve immediately.

SERVES: 4 | PREP TIME: 25 MINS | COOKING TIME: 2 MINS

Crispy Sesame Chicken Noodle Salad

30 g / 1 oz / ½ cup dried wood ear fungus
400 g / 14 oz wide flat rice noodles
1 carrot, julienned
1 yellow pepper, deseeded and julienned
1 leek, sliced
150 g / 5 ½ oz / 1 cup sugar snap peas
75 g / 2 ½ oz / ½ cup peas, defrosted
  if frozen
1 tbsp caster (superfine) sugar
1 lime, juiced, plus extra wedges to serve
1 tbsp fish sauce
2 tbsp spring onion (scallion)
  greens, chopped
1 red chilli (chili), sliced
300 g / 10 ½ oz / 2 cups crispy
  sesame chicken
1 tbsp sesame seeds

1. Soak the fungus in cold water for 20 minutes, then drain well.
2. Meanwhile, cook the noodles according to the packet instructions, then drain and plunge into iced water. Drain well.
3. Blanch the vegetables in boiling salted water for 2 minutes, then drain and plunge into iced water. Drain well.
4. Divide the noodles, fungus and vegetables between four bowls.
5. Stir the sugar into the lime juice and fish sauce until it dissolves, then drizzle it over the salads and scatter with spring onion greens and chillies.
6. Arrange the chicken on top and sprinkle with sesame seeds.

SERVES: 4 | PREP TIME: 45 MINS | COOKING TIME: 20 MINS

Meatball Noodles with Pineapple

450 g / 1 lb / 3 cups minced pork
1 tsp fresh root ginger, finely grated
4 spring onions (scallions), whites finely chopped, greens sliced
50 ml / 1 ¾ fl. oz / ¼ cup shaoxing rice wine
3 tbsp kecap manis
1 tbsp sesame oil
3 medium eggs, beaten
1 tbsp cornflour (cornstarch)
100 g / 3 ½ oz / 1 cup panko breadcrumbs
2 tbsp vegetable oil
30 g / 1 oz / ¼ cup cashew nuts
1 large red chilli (chili), sliced
400 g / 14 fl. oz / 2 cups canned pineapple chunks in juice
400 g / 14 oz flat wheat noodles
sesame seeds and coriander (cilantro) leaves, to serve

1. Put the pork in a large mixing bowl and beat in 60 ml of cold water. Add the ginger and spring onion whites and mix well.

2. Whisk the rice wine with the kecap manis, sesame oil and eggs, then slowly incorporate it into the pork mixture. Mix the cornflour with the breadcrumbs, then work it into the pork.

3. Shape the mixture into 16 meatballs, then cover and chill in the fridge for 30 minutes.

4. Heat the vegetable oil in a frying pan and sear the meatballs until browned all over.

5. Add the cashew nuts and chilli and cook until the cashews are golden brown. Add the pineapple and its juice, then cover and simmer for 5 minutes.

6. Meanwhile, cook the noodles according to the packet instructions. Toss the noodles with the meatballs and sauce and serve garnished with sesame seeds and coriander leaves.

Pork and Bamboo Shoot Siu Mai

175 g / 6 oz / 1 ¼ cups plain
 (all-purpose) flour
225 g / 8 oz / 1 ½ cups minced pork
2 spring onions (scallions), finely chopped
1 tsp fresh root ginger, finely grated
100 g / 3 ½ oz / ½ cup canned bamboo
 shoots, finely chopped
1 tbsp light soy sauce
1 tsp caster (superfine) sugar
1 tsp sesame oil
1 tsp cornflour (cornstarch)
1 egg white, beaten
2 tbsp crab roe (optional)

1. Sift the flour into a bowl and stir in 160 ml of recently boiled water. Knead for
   8 minutes or until smooth, adding more flour if necessary. Rest for 30 minutes.
2. Meanwhile, mix the pork with the spring onions, ginger, bamboo shoots, soy sauce,
   sugar, sesame oil and cornflour. Season with 1 teaspoon of salt and some freshly
   ground white pepper.
3. Divide the rested dough into 24 balls, then roll out each one into a 7.5 cm (3 in)
   circle on a floured surface.
4. Put a heaped teaspoon of filling in the centre of each circle, then brush round the
   edge with egg white. Gather up the edges and twist round to seal, leaving a small
   opening at the top. Add a small piece of crab roe to the top of each one, if using.
5. Space out the siu mai in oiled steamer baskets and steam for 10 minutes, then
   serve immediately.

Singapore Noodles with Chicken

400 g / 14 oz thin rice noodles
2 tbsp vegetable oil
1 skinless chicken breast, cut into chunks
2 red chillies (chilies), sliced diagonally
¼ savoy cabbage, sliced
1 large carrot, peeled and coarsely grated
2 tbsp curry powder
50 ml / 1 ¾ fl. oz / ¼ cup shaoxing rice wine
2 tbsp light soy sauce
1 tsp sesame oil

1. Soak the noodles according to the packet instructions, then drain well.
2. Heat the oil in a large wok and fry the chicken until it loses its raw look.
3. Add the chillies, cabbage and carrot and stir-fry for 2 minutes.
4. Add the noodles, then sprinkle the curry powder evenly over the top and toss well.
5. Add the rice wine, soy sauce and sesame oil and stir-fry for 1 minute, then divide
   between four warm bowls and serve immediately.

SERVES: 4 | PREP TIME: 15 MINS | COOKING TIME: 10 MINS

Crispy Chilli Beef

175 ml / 6 fl. oz / ⅔ cup pineapple juice
100 ml / 3 ½ fl. oz / ½ cup sweet
  chilli sauce
1 tbsp light soy sauce
vegetable oil, for deep-frying
450 g / 1 lb / 3 cups minute steak,
  very thinly sliced
1 tsp five spice powder
100 g / 3 ½ oz / ⅔ cup cornflour
  (cornstarch)
2 spring onions (scallions), sliced

1. To make the sauce, put the pineapple juice, chilli sauce and soy sauce in a small saucepan. Bring to the boil and cook until it has reduced enough to coat the back of the spoon.

2. Season the beef with salt and five spice, then toss it with the cornflour, squeezing to ensure it adheres well.

3. Heat the oil in a deep fat fryer, according to the manufacturer's instructions, to a temperature of 180°C (350F).

4. Deep fry the beef in two batches for 4 minutes or until very crisp. Drain the beef on plenty of kitchen paper, then toss it with the sauce.

5. Sprinkle the beef with spring onions and serve immediately.

MAKES: 16 | PREP TIME: 20 MINS | COOKING TIME: 4 MINS

Crispy Duck Rolls

½ Cantonese roast duck, boned, shredded and cooled
2 tbsp hoisin sauce
4 spring onions (scallions), finely julienned
200 g / 7 oz / 1 cup canned bamboo shoots, drained and finely julienned
16 small spring roll wrappers
1 tsp cornflour, mixed with 1 tbsp boiling water

1. Mix the duck with the hoisin, spring onions and bamboo shoots.
2. Divide the mixture between the spring roll wrappers. Fold up the bottom corner, then fold in the sides. Brush the top corner with some of the cornflour glue, then roll them up tightly into a cigar shape.
3. Heat the vegetable oil in a deep fat fryer, according to the manufacturer's instructions, to a temperature of 180°C (350F).
4. Fry the rolls in batches for 4 minutes or until golden and crisp.
5. Drain on plenty of kitchen paper and serve immediately.

MAKES: **32** | PREP TIME: **1 HOUR** | COOKING TIME: **10 MINS**

Pork and Courgette Jiaozi

175 g / 6 oz / 1 ¼ cups plain (all-purpose) flour
225 g / 8 oz / 1 ½ cups minced pork
2 tbsp dark soy sauce
1 tbsp shaoxing rice wine
1 tsp sesame oil
1 egg, separated
225 g / 8 oz / 1 ¾ cups courgette (zucchini), coarsely grated
100 g / 3 ½ oz / 2 cups chives, finely chopped, plus extra to garnish
½ tbsp fresh root ginger, finely grated
1 tbsp vegetable oil
3 clove of garlic, finely chopped
1 tbsp light soy sauce

1. Stir 160 ml of recently boiled water into the flour, then knead for 8 minutes. Rest for 30 minutes.
2. Meanwhile, mix the pork with 50 ml cold water, then beat in the dark soy, rice wine, sesame oil and egg yolk. Stir in the courgette, chives and ginger.
3. Roll the dough into thirty 7.5 cm (3 in) circles. Lay one circle on a dumpling press and add a heaped teaspoon of filling. Brush the edges with egg white, then fold in half and squeeze to seal. Repeat to make 32.
4. Boil a large saucepan of water. Add half of the dumplings and stir well. Cover and return to the boil, then add 250 ml of cold water. Repeat twice more, then remove the dumplings from the pan with a slotted spoon. Repeat the process with the rest of the dumplings.
5. Heat the vegetable oil and fry the garlic for 1 minute, then stir in the soy sauce. Divide the dumplings between warm plates and top with the fried garlic and a sprinkle of chives.

SERVES: 4 | PREP TIME: 10 MINS | MARINATE: OVERNIGHT | COOKING: 10 MINS

Sticky Pork Noodles

2 tbsp hoisin sauce
2 tbsp sweet soy sauce or kecap manis
2 tbsp runny honey
1 tsp five spice powder
1 tsp sesame oil
450 g / 1 lb / 3 cups pork loin, cubed
400 g / 14 oz medium egg noodles
2 tbsp vegetable oil
2 cloves of garlic, crushed
2 tsp fresh root ginger, finely grated
1 red onion, thinly sliced
1 carrot, julienned
2 spring onions (scallions), julienned

1. Put the hoisin, soy, honey, five spice and sesame oil in a saucepan. Stir continuously while it comes to the boil, then leave to cool. Scrape the mixture into a freezer bag, add the pork and massage well to coat. Marinate in the fridge overnight.

2. Cook the noodles according to the packet instructions, then drain and plunge into iced water. Drain well.

3. Remove the pork from the freezer bag and reserve the marinade.

4. Heat the vegetable oil in a wok and fry the garlic and ginger for 30 seconds. Add the onion and stir-fry for 1 minute.

5. Add the pork and stir fry for 4 minutes or until lightly coloured. Add the carrot and noodles and stir fry for 2 minutes. Pour in the reserved marinade, then cover and cook for 2 minutes.

6. Toss in the spring onions, then divide between four warm plates and serve immediately.

Fish Dishes

SERVES: 4 | PREP TIME: 5 MINS | COOKING TIME: 5 MINS

Eel with Honey Pepper Sauce

200 ml / 7 fl. oz / ¾ cup runny honey
75 ml / 2 ½ fl. oz / ⅓ cup dark soy sauce
75 ml / 2 ½ fl. oz / ⅓ cup pineapple juice
2 tbsp rice wine vinegar
1 tsp freshly ground black pepper
1 clove of garlic, crushed
1 lemon, juiced
1 large eel, skinned, filleted and halved
1 tbsp sesame seeds
steamed rice, to serve

1. Put the honey, soy, pineapple juice, vinegar, black pepper, garlic and lemon juice in a small saucepan. Stir over a low heat until it starts to simmer, then cook gently for 5 minutes or until syrupy.

2. Meanwhile, cook the eel fillets under a hot grill for 2 minutes on each side or until just cooked in the centre. Transfer to a chopping board and slice on the diagonal.

3. Serve the eel on a bed of rice. Spoon over the sauce and sprinkle with sesame seeds.

Salt and Pepper Whitebait

sunflower oil, for deep frying
75 g / 2 ½ oz / ½ cup plain (all-purpose) flour
75 g / 2 ½ oz / ½ cup potato starch
1 tsp chilli (chili) powder
1 tsp ground Szechwan peppercorns
1 tsp ground black peppercorns
450 g / 1 lb / 3 cups fresh whitebait

1. Heat the oil in a deep fat fryer, according to the manufacturer's instructions, to a temperature of 180°C (350F).
2. Mix the flour with the potato starch, chilli powder, Szechwan and black pepper and 1 teaspoon of salt. Toss the whitebait with the flour mixture to coat and shake off any excess.
3. Deep-fry in batches for 5 minutes or until crisp.
4. Transfer the whitebait to a kitchen paper lined bowl to remove any excess oil, then serve immediately.

MAKES: 36 | PREP TIME: 45 MINS | COOKING TIME: 10 MINS

Cheong Fun

125 g / 4 ½ oz / ½ cup dried shrimps
250 g / 9 oz / 1 ⅔ cups white rice flour
75 g / 2 ½ oz / ½ cup tapioca flour
40 g / 1 ½ oz / ¼ cup cornflour (cornstarch)
50 ml / 1 ¾ fl. oz / ¼ cup vegetable oil, plus extra for brushing
3 mild red chillies (chilies), deseeded and thinly julienned
1 bunch chives, half cut into short lengths, half chopped
chilli (chili) oil, for dipping

1. Soak the shrimps in cold water for 1 hour, then drain and dry thoroughly with kitchen paper.
2. Mix the three flours together, then rub in the oil. Gradually incorporate 900 ml of cold water to make a batter.
3. Line a small rectangular baking tray that will fit inside your steamer with a layer of wet muslin and preheat the steamer to high. Brush a large chopping board with oil.
4. Ladle enough batter into the tray to cover the bottom, then sprinkle with some of the prawns, chillies and short chive lengths. Cover and steam for 3 minutes or until set and opaque.
5. Use a silicone spatula to prise the cheong fun away from the muslin, rolling it up as you go, then transfer to the chopping board, brush with oil and cut into short lengths.
6. Repeat until all of the batter has been used, then sprinkle with chopped chives and serve, with chilli oil for dipping.

SERVES: 1 | **PREP TIME: 15 MINS** | **COOKING TIME: 5 MINS**

Crispy Noodles with Seafood

1 small squid tube, cleaned
100 g / 3 ½ oz / 1 cup thin egg noodles
vegetable oil, for deep frying
1 tbsp sunflower oil
2 dried red chillies (chilies)
3 raw king prawns, peeled
1 handful mangetout
3 pak choi leaves
1 tbsp light soy sauce

1. Open out the squid tube and score the inside with a sharp knife in a fine diamond pattern. Cut it into five pieces and set aside.
2. Blanch the noodles in boiling water for 2 minutes, then drain well. Spread them out on a clean tea towel and dry thoroughly with kitchen paper.
3. Heat the vegetable oil in a deep fat fryer, according to the manufacturer's instructions, to a temperature of 180°C (350F). Deep fry the noodles for 1 minute or until golden and crisp. Drain well on plenty of kitchen paper and keep warm in a low oven.
4. Heat the sunflower oil in a wok and fry the chillies and prawns for 1 minute. Add the mangetout and cook for 1 minute, then add the squid and pak choi. As soon as the squid curls up and turns opaque, season with soy sauce and take the wok off the heat.
5. Serve the seafood and vegetables on top of the noodles immediately.

Prawn Noodle Salad

30 g / 1 oz / ½ cup dried wood ear fungus
400 g / 14 oz vermicelli rice noodles
150 g / 5 ½ oz / 1 cup sugar snap peas
½ red pepper, deseeded and chopped
½ yellow pepper, deseeded and chopped
½ carrot, peeled and julienned
½ spring onion, finely chopped
1 handful bean sprouts
75 g / 2 ½ oz / ½ cup frozen peas, defrosted
12 cooked king prawns
1 lime, juiced
1 tbsp soy sauce
1 tbsp caster (superfine) sugar
1 tbsp sesame oil

1. Soak the fungus in cold water for 20 minutes, then drain and thinly slice.
2. Meanwhile, cook the noodles according to the packet instructions, then drain and plunge into iced water. Drain well.
3. Blanch the sugar snap peas in boiling water for 3 minutes, then plunge into iced water and drain well.
4. Toss the noodles with the fungus, vegetables and prawns.
5. Mix the lime juice with the soy sauce, sugar and sesame oil, then toss the dressing with the salad. Refrigerate until you are ready to serve.

Crispy King Prawns

vegetable oil, for deep frying
75 g / 2 ½ oz / ½ cup plain
   (all-purpose) flour
1 large egg, separated
150 ml / 5 ½ fl. oz / ⅔ cup sparkling water
300 g / 10 ½ oz / 2 cups raw king prawns,
   peeled with tails left intact
lemon slices and chopped parsley, to serve

1. Heat the oil in a deep fat fryer, according to the manufacturer's instructions, to a temperature of 190°C (375F).
2. Put 60 g of flour in a bowl and make a well in the middle. Add the egg yolk and sparkling water, then whisk them together, gradually incorporating all the flour from round the outside. Whip the egg white until stiff, then fold it into the batter.
3. Toss the prawns with the rest of the flour and shake off any excess. Working in batches, dip the prawns in the batter, then deep-fry for 2 minutes or until crisp.
4. Drain on plenty of kitchen paper and serve immediately, garnished with lemon and parsley.

Octopus Noodle Salad

50 ml / 1 ¾ fl. oz / ¼ cup dark soy sauce
5 cm (2 in) fresh root ginger, sliced
1 bulb garlic, halved horizontally
1 octopus, frozen for at least 2 weeks
 and defrosted
400 g / 14 oz glass noodles
1 carrot, julienned
1 yellow pepper, deseeded
 and julienned
1 leek, sliced

150 g / 5 ½ oz / 1 cup sugar snap peas
75 g / 2 ½ oz / ½ cup peas, defrosted
 if frozen
1 tbsp caster (superfine) sugar
1 lime, juiced, plus extra wedges to serve
1 tbsp fish sauce
1 tbsp chives, chopped
1 tbsp sesame seeds

1. Bring a large saucepan of water to the boil and stir in the dark soy, ginger and garlic. Submerge the octopus and simmer for 50 minutes or until tender.
2. Meanwhile, cook the noodles according to the packet instructions, then drain and plunge into iced water. Drain well.
3. Blanch the vegetables in boiling salted water for 2 minutes, then drain and plunge into iced water. Drain well
4. Divide the noodles and vegetables between four bowls. Discard the eyes and beak of the octopus and slice the rest, then arrange on top.
5. Stir the sugar into the lime juice and fish sauce until it dissolves, then drizzle it over the salads. Serve sprinkled with chives and sesame seeds.

Tomato and Garlic King Prawns

1 tbsp vegetable oil
2 cloves of garlic, sliced
3 medium tomatoes, diced
75 ml / 2 ½ fl. oz / ⅓ cup shaoxing
   rice wine
1 tbsp light soy sauce
vegetable oil, for deep frying
75 g / 2 ½ oz / ½ cup cornflour (cornstarch)
300 g / 10 ½ oz / 2 cups raw king prawns,
   peeled with tails left intact
thyme and rosemary, to garnish

1. Heat 1 tablespoon of oil in a wok and fry the garlic for 1 minute. Add the tomatoes and rice wine and simmer for 2 minutes. Season to taste with soy sauce and set aside.
2. Heat the oil in a deep fat fryer, according to the manufacturer's instructions, to a temperature of 190°C (375F).
3. Toss the prawns with the cornflour and shake off any excess. Deep-fry in batches for 2 minutes or until crisp.
4. Drain on plenty of kitchen paper, then toss with the sauce and serve immediately, garnished with thyme and rosemary.

Prawn and Bamboo Shoot Wonton Soup

225 g / 8 oz / 1 ½ cups raw prawns
   (shrimp), chopped
75 g / 2 ½ oz / ⅔ cup bamboo shoots,
   finely chopped
2 spring onions (scallions), whites finely
   chopped, greens sliced
1 tsp fresh root ginger, finely grated
1 tsp shaoxing rice wine
1 tsp caster (superfine) sugar
1 tsp sesame oil
1 tsp cornflour (cornstarch)
24 wonton wrappers
1 egg white, beaten
1 litre / 17 ½ fl. oz / 4 cups clear fish stock
1 tbsp soy sauce
1 handful fresh coriander (cilantro) leaves

1. Mix the chopped prawns with the bamboo shoots, spring onion whites, ginger, rice wine, sugar, sesame oil and cornflour. Season with 1 teaspoon of salt and some freshly ground white pepper.
2. Add a teaspoon of the mixture to the centre of each wonton wrapper. Brush round the outside with egg white, then draw up the sides of each wrapper and squeeze just above the filling to make a sack shape.
3. Bring the stock to a simmer in a large saucepan. Add the wontons and poach for 4 minutes.
4. Divide the soup and wontons between four bowls and garnish with spring onion greens and coriander leaves.

SERVES: **4** | PREP TIME: **15 MINS** | COOKING TIME: **8 MINS**

Spicy Seafood Soup

3 medium squid tubes
3 red chillies (chilies), sliced, plus extra
    to garnish
2 cloves of garlic, chopped
1 tbsp vegetable oil
1 tbsp fresh root ginger, very thinly sliced
2 stalks lemongrass, bruised
3 spring onions (scallions), whites
    chopped, greens cut into short lengths
1 litre / 1 pint 14 fl. oz / 4 cups fish stock
2 tbsp shaoxing rice wine
2 tsp caster (superfine) sugar
1 tbsp light soy sauce
200 g / 7 oz / 1 cup canned straw
    mushrooms, drained
12 raw king prawns, peeled with tails
    left intact
8 green lip mussels in the half-shell,
    defrosted if frozen
lime juice and chopped fresh coriander
    (cilantro), to serve

1. Open out the squid tubes, then score
   the inside with a sharp knife in a
   diamond pattern. Cut into bite-sized
   chunks and set aside.

2. Pound the chillies in a pestle and
   mortar with a pinch of salt to a fine
   paste. Add the garlic and pound again.

3. Heat the oil in a large wok and stir-fry
   the paste with the ginger, lemongrass
   and spring onion whites for 2 minutes.
   Add the stock, rice wine, sugar and
   soy sauce and bring to the boil.

4. Add the mushrooms, prawns and
   mussels and poach until the prawns
   turn opaque. Add the squid and
   poach until the pieces curl up and
   turn opaque.

5. Season the soup to taste with lime
   juice and salt, then ladle into bowls
   and garnish with spring onion greens
   and chopped coriander.

SERVES: **4** | PREP TIME: **10 MINS** | COOKING TIME: **5 MINS**

Squid with Black Bean sauce

4 large squid tubes, cleaned
2 tbsp vegetable oil
2 cloves of garlic, finely chopped
1 tbsp root ginger, finely chopped
2 spring onions (scallions), cut into
   short lengths
2 red chillies (chilies), sliced
2 tbsp fermented black beans, rinsed
   and mashed
2 tbsp shaoxing rice wine
1 tbsp dark soy sauce
1 tbsp oyster sauce
½ tsp cornflour (cornstarch)
steamed rice, to serve
1 handful fresh coriander
   (cilantro), chopped

1. Open out the squid tubes and score
   the inside at 3 mm intervals. Cut the
   squid into bite sized pieces and
   set aside.
2. Heat the vegetable oil in a large wok
   and fry the garlic and ginger for
   1 minute. Add the spring onions,
   chillies and black beans and fry for
   1 minute.
3. Add the rice wine, soy and oyster
   sauce and stir well. Slake the cornflour
   with 3 tablespoons of cold water, add
   it to the pan and stir until thickened.
4. Add the squid and stir-fry for 1 minute
   or until it curls up and turns opaque.
5. Serve immediately on a bed of rice,
   sprinkled with coriander.

SERVES: **4** | PREP TIME: **15 MINS** | MARINATE: **1 HOUR** | COOKING TIME: **6 MINS**

Barbecued Red Mullet

2 tbsp light soy sauce
2 lemons, 1 juiced, 1 halved and sliced
2 tbsp runny honey
50 ml / 1 ¾ fl. oz / ¼ cup shaoxing rice wine
1 tsp sesame oil
8 red mullet, gutted and scaled
2 tbsp vegetable oil

1. Whisk the soy sauce with the lemon juice, honey, rice wine and sesame oil. Pour the mixture over the fish, then marinate in the fridge for 1 hour.
2. Dry the mullet thoroughly with kitchen paper, then brush with oil and season liberally with salt and pepper. This will help to prevent them from sticking. Add a slice of lemon to the belly cavity of each one.
3. Make sure the metal barbecue grill is very hot before adding the fish. Cook over medium-hot coals for 3 minutes on each side or until the skin is brown and blistered and the flesh pulls easily away from the bones at the thickest part by the head.

Summer Rolls

75 g / 2 ½ oz vermicelli rice noodles
6 rice paper wrappers
18 cooked king prawns, peeled
6 soft lettuce leaves
¼ cucumber, julienned
½ carrot, coarsely grated
soy sauce, for dipping

1. Put the noodles in a bowl and pour over enough boiling water to cover by 5 cm (2 in). Leave to soak for 4 minutes, then drain well.
2. Dip the first rice paper wrapper in a bowl of cold water, then lay it out on a clean chopping board. Arrange three prawns across the middle, then lay a lettuce leaf on top and add some noodles, cucumber and carrot.
3. Fold over the sides of the wrapper, then roll it up to enclose the filling.
4. Repeat with the rest of the ingredients to form six rolls, then serve immediately with soy sauce for dipping.

Steamed Eggs with Prawns

2 large eggs
100 ml / 3 ½ fl. oz / ½ cup fish stock
½ tsp fresh root ginger, finely grated
3 raw king prawns, butterflied
coriander (cilantro) leaves, to garnish

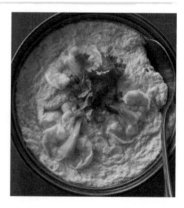

1. Whisk the eggs with the fish stock and a pinch of salt in a small heatproof bowl.
2. Transfer the bowl to a steamer and steam for 7 minutes.
3. Sprinkle with ginger and add the prawns, then cover and steam again for 3 minutes or until the egg has set.
4. Serve immediately.

Deep-fried Soft Shell Crabs

2 tbsp vegetable oil, plus extra for deep frying
75 g / 2 ½ oz / ½ cup plain (all-purpose) flour
1 large egg, separated
150 ml / 5 ½ fl. oz / ⅔ cup sparkling water
8 soft shell crabs, cleaned and trimmed
8 kaffir lime leaves
1 large red chilli (chili), deseeded and sliced
2 cloves of garlic, sliced
50 g / 1 ¾ oz / ⅔ cup fresh green peppercorns

1. Heat the oil in a deep fat fryer, according to the manufacturer's instructions, to a temperature of 180°C (350F).
2. Put 60 g of flour in a bowl and make a well in the middle. Add the egg yolk and sparkling water, then whisk them together, gradually incorporating all the flour from round the outside. Whip the egg white until stiff, then fold it into the batter.
3. Toss the crabs with the rest of the flour and shake off any excess. Working in batches, dip the crabs in the batter, then deep-fry for 3 minutes or until crisp. Drain on plenty of kitchen paper.
4. Heat 2 tablespoons of oil in a large wok and fry the lime leaves, chilli, garlic and peppercorns for 1 minute or until fragrant. Season with salt and white pepper, then serve immediately with your favourite dipping sauce.

MAKES: 24 | PREP TIME: 30 MINS | COOKING TIME: 8 MINS

Steamed Prawn Wontons

225 g / 8 oz / 1 ½ cups raw prawns (shrimp), chopped
2 canned water chestnuts, finely chopped
1 tsp fresh root ginger, finely grated
1 tsp shaoxing rice wine
1 tsp caster (superfine) sugar
1 tsp sesame oil
1 tsp cornflour (cornstarch)
24 wonton wrappers
1 egg white, beaten
¼ Chinese cabbage, cubed (optional)

1. Mix the chopped prawns with the water chestnuts, ginger, rice wine, sugar, sesame oil and cornflour. Season with 1 teaspoon of salt and some freshly ground white pepper.
2. Add a teaspoon of the mixture to the centre of each wonton wrapper. Brush round the outside with egg white, then draw up the sides of each wrapper and squeeze just above the filling to make a sack shape.
3. Space out the wontons in oiled steamer baskets, adding some Chinese cabbage to each if you prefer.
4. Steam the wontons for 8 minutes, then serve immediately.

SERVES: **4** | PREP TIME: **5 MINS** | COOKING TIME: **20 MINS**

Spicy Prawn Noodle Stir Fry

400 g / 14 oz thin egg noodles
2 tbsp sunflower oil
3 cloves of garlic, finely chopped
1 tbsp fresh root ginger, finely chopped
2 red chillies (chilies), finely chopped
½ tsp dried red chilli (chili) flakes
½ red pepper, quartered, deseeded and thinly sliced
½ yellow pepper, quartered, deseeded and thinly sliced
½ green pepper, quartered, deseeded and thinly sliced
300 g / 10 ½ oz / 2 cups raw king prawns, peeled
50 ml / 1 ¾ fl. oz / ¼ cup shaoxing rice wine
2 tbsp soy sauce
1 tsp sesame oil
2 tbsp peanuts, finely chopped

1. Cook the noodles according to the packet instructions, then drain and plunge into iced water. Drain well.
2. Heat the oil in a large wok and fry the garlic, ginger, chillies and chilli flakes for 3 minutes.
3. Add the peppers and prawns and stir-fry for 5 minutes or until the prawns have turned opaque.
4. Add the rice wine, soy and sesame oil and heat until it starts to simmer, then stir in the noodles. Stir fry for 2 more minutes, then serve straight away, sprinkled with peanuts.

MAKES: **12** | PREP TIME: **30 MINS** | COOKING TIME: **15 MINS**

Baked Scallop Wontons

150 g / 5 ½ oz / 1 cup raw prawns
  (shrimp), finely chopped
1 tsp fresh root ginger, finely grated
1 spring onion (scallion), very
  finely chopped
1 tsp shaoxing rice wine
1 tsp caster (superfine) sugar
1 tsp cornflour (cornstarch)
12 fresh scallops, shelled and cleaned
24 wonton wrappers
1 egg white, beaten
2 tbsp vegetable oil
chives, to garnish

1. Preheat the oven to 200°C (180°C fan)
   / 400F / gas 6.
2. Mix the chopped prawns with the
   ginger, spring onion, rice wine, sugar
   and cornflour. Season with ½ a
   teaspoon of salt and some freshly
   ground white pepper.
3. Divide the prawn mixture into
   twelve and shape each piece around
   a scallop.
4. Brush the wonton wrappers with egg
   white and wrap two around each
   scallop to completely enclose.
5. Brush the wontons with oil and space
   them out on an oiled baking tray.
6. Bake the wontons for 15 minutes or
   until pale brown and crisp.
   The scallops should only just
   be cooked in the centre.
7. Serve immediately, garnished
   with chives.

Open Crab Dim Sum

100 g / 3 ½ oz / ⅔ cup white crab meat
75 g / 2 ½ oz / ½ cup raw prawns, chopped
½ carrot, peeled and grated
1 red chilli (chili), finely chopped
1 tsp fresh root ginger, finely grated
2 tsp light soy sauce
1 tsp caster (superfine) sugar
1 tsp sesame oil
1 tsp cornflour (cornstarch)
24 round wonton wrappers
100 g / 3 ½ oz / ⅔ cup brown crab meat
chives, to garnish

1. Preheat the oven to 220°C (200°C fan) / 425F / gas 7 and oil a 24-hole mini muffin tin that will fit inside a roasting tin.
2. Mix the white crab meat and prawns with the carrot, chilli, ginger, soy sauce, sugar, sesame oil and cornflour.
3. Add a spoonful of brown crab meat to the centre of each wonton wrapper and spread it into a circle. Top each one with a spoonful of filling, then transfer them to the mini muffin tin, allowing the edges to pleat in like the petals of a flower.
4. Add 2.5 cm (1 in) of boiling water to the roasting tin and carefully lower in the muffin tin. Cover the roasting tin tightly with foil, then transfer to the oven to steam for 12 minutes, or until the wrappers are cooked.
5. Serve the dim sum sprinkled with chives.

Prawn and Spinach Soup

2 tbsp vegetable oil
2 cloves of garlic, finely chopped
2 tsp fresh root ginger, finely chopped
4 spring onions (scallions), chopped
2 tbsp shaoxing rice wine
1 tsp caster (superfine) sugar
1 litre / 1 pint 14 fl. oz / 4 cups fish stock
100 g / 3 ½ oz / 3 cups spinach, washed
200 g / 7 oz / 1 ⅓ cups sugar snap peas
12 large king prawns, heads removed
1 tbsp dark soy sauce
1 handful fresh coriander (cilantro) leaves

1. Heat the oil in a large wok and fry the garlic, ginger and spring onions for 2 minutes. Add the rice wine and sugar and stir-fry for 1 minute.
2. Add the fish stock and bring to the boil, then add the spinach. Cook for 1 minute, then blend until smooth in a liquidizer.
3. Return the soup to the wok and add the sugar snaps and prawns.
4. Simmer for 5 minutes, then season to taste with soy sauce.
5. Garnish with coriander and serve immediately.

SERVES: 6 | **PREP TIME: 15 MINS** | **COOKING TIME: 3 MINS**

Sunflower Prawn Toasts

150 g / 5 ½ oz / 1 cup raw prawns (shrimp), peeled
1 clove of garlic, crushed
1 tsp fresh root ginger, finely grated
½ tsp chilli (chili) paste
1 tbsp white rice flour
1 egg yolk
1 tsp soy sauce
1 tsp sesame oil
6 slices white bread
50 g / 1 ¾ oz / ⅓ cup sunflower seeds
sunflower oil, for deep frying
spring onion (scallion) greens, to garnish

1. Put the prawns in a food processor with the garlic, ginger, chilli paste, rice flour, egg yolk, soy and sesame oil. Blend to a paste.
2. Divide the paste between the slices of bread and spread into an even layer. Cut each slice into four triangles.
3. Heat the oil in a deep fat fryer, according to the manufacturer's instructions, to a temperature of 180°C (350F).
4. Dip the prawn layer in sunflower seeds to coat, then fry the toasts in batches for 3 minutes, turning them over halfway through.
5. Drain on plenty of kitchen paper, then serve immediately, garnished with spring onion greens.

SERVES: 6 | PREP TIME: 5 MINS | COOKING TIME: 1 HOUR 10 MINS

Prawn Congee

200 g / 7 oz / 1 cup jasmine rice
2.3 litres / 4 pints / 8 cups fish stock
2 tbsp dried shrimps
300 g / 10 ½ oz / 2 cups raw king prawns,
  peeled and deveined
75 ml / 2 ½ fl. oz / ⅓ cup vegetable oil
2 cloves of garlic, finely chopped
2 spring onions (scallions), whites finely
  chopped, greens cut into 2 cm lengths
75 g / 2 ½ oz / 1 cup fresh
  white breadcrumbs
1 tbsp fresh root ginger, coarsely grated
1 small bunch fresh coriander (cilantro),
  roughly chopped

1. Put the rice and all but 300 ml of
   the stock in a saucepan with ½ a
   teaspoon of salt. Bring the mixture
   to the boil, then reduce the heat and
   simmer for 1 hour or until the rice has
   broken down into a thick porridge,
   stirring occasionally.

2. Meanwhile, soak the dried shrimps in
   hot water for 30 minutes, then drain
   and dry well.

3. When the rice is ready, bring the rest
   of the stock to the boil in a small
   saucepan. Gently poach the prawns
   until they turn opaque, then strain the
   stock into the congee pan and stir
   well. Taste and adjust the seasoning
   with salt and white pepper if necessary.

4. Heat the vegetable oil in a wok and
   fry the garlic, spring onion whites and
   rehydrated shrimps for 1 minute.

5. Add the breadcrumbs and stir-fry
   until golden and crisp.

6. Ladle the congee into six bowls and
   top with the prawns and breadcrumb
   mixture. Garnish with grated ginger,
   spring onion greens and fresh
   coriander.

SERVES: 6 | PREP TIME: 10 MINS | COOKING TIME: 10 MINS

Crab, Pork and Noodle Soup

300 g / 10 ½ oz / 2 cups coarsely minced pork
200 g / 7 oz / 1 ⅓ cups crab meat (50/50 white and brown)
1 tsp red curry paste
3 large eggs, beaten
450 g / 1 lb thin rice noodles
1 tbsp vegetable oil
3 spring onions (scallions), finely chopped, white and green parts separated
2 cloves of garlic, finely chopped
3 medium tomatoes, diced
1 tbsp fish sauce
1 tbsp tamarind paste
holy basil, to garnish

1. Beat the pork in a bowl with the crab, curry paste, eggs and 1 teaspoon of salt. Set aside.
2. Cook the noodles according to the packet instructions or until al dente. Plunge into cold water, then drain well.
3. Heat the oil in a large wok and fry the spring onion whites and garlic for 1 minute. Add the tomatoes and fish sauce and stir-fry for 2 minutes. Pour in 1.5 litres of boiling water and stir in the tamarind and 1 teaspoon of salt.
4. Scoop spoonfuls of the pork mixture into the boiling liquid. When it rises to the surface, stir in the noodles and taste the soup for seasoning.
5. Divide the soup between six bowls and garnish with spring onion greens and holy basil.

Instant Noodles with Chilli Paste

300 ml / 10 ½ fl. oz / 1 ¼ cup vegetable oil
6 cloves of garlic, finely chopped
1 tbsp fresh root ginger, finely chopped
50 g / 1 ¾ oz / ⅓ cup chilli (chili) flakes
25 g tiny dried shrimps, rinsed and
  dried (optional)
1 ½ tbsp soy sauce
1 tbsp runny honey
1 litre / 17 ½ fl. oz / 4 cups vegetable stock
300 g / 10 ½ oz / 4 blocks plain
  instant noodles
2 pak choi, halved
1 large tomato, sliced
2 salted duck eggs, halved
1 mild red chilli (chili), sliced

1. To make the chilli paste, heat the oil in a wok and fry the garlic and ginger for
   2 minutes or until fragrant, but not coloured. Add the dried shrimps and fry for
   1 minute.
2. Stir in ½ a teaspoon of salt, then take the pan off the heat and leave to cool for 30
   seconds. Stir in the chilli flakes, followed by the soy sauce and honey. Transfer to a
   serving bowl and leave to cool.
3. Place a block of instant noodles in each of four bowls. Smear the top of each block
   with a heaped teaspoon of the chilli paste and add a few slices of tomato, half a pak
   choi and half a salted duck egg to each one. Garnish with sliced chilli.
4. Cover the noodles with boiling water and leave to soften for 4 minutes, or
   according to the packet instructions, before serving.

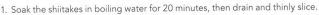

Prawn and Shiitake Salad

30 g / 1 oz / ½ cup dried shiitake
  mushrooms
400 g / 14 oz flat rice noodles
200 g / 7 oz / 1 ⅓ cups cooked prawns
  (shrimp), peeled
4 spring onions (scallions), sliced
1 red chilli (chili), sliced
1 green chilli (chili), sliced
4 sprigs mint
1 tbsp caster (superfine) sugar
1 lime, juiced, plus extra wedges to serve
1 tbsp fish sauce

1. Soak the shiitakes in boiling water for 20 minutes, then drain and thinly slice.
2. Meanwhile, cook the noodles according to the packet instructions, then drain and
   plunge into iced water. Drain well.
3. Divide the noodles between four bowls and top with the prawns, spring onions,
   chillies and mint.
4. Stir the sugar into the lime juice and fish sauce until it dissolves, then drizzle it over
   the salads. Serve immediately, with extra wedges of lime on the side.

SERVES: 4 | PREP TIME: 5 MINS | MARINATE: 1 HOUR | COOKING TIME: 4 MINS

Low Fat Prawn Toasts

100 g / 3 ½ oz / ⅔ cup cooked prawns (shrimp), peeled
1 clove of garlic, squashed
2 slices fresh root ginger
1 lime, juiced
1 tsp caster (superfine) sugar
1 tbsp light soy sauce
4 slices baguette
2 tsp sesame oil
dill sprigs, to garnish

1. Put the prawns in a bowl with the garlic, ginger, lime juice, sugar and soy sauce. Cover and leave to marinate in the fridge for 1 hour.
2. Toast the baguette slices on both sides under a hot grill, then brush them with sesame oil.
3. Drain the prawns and discard the garlic and ginger. Pile the prawns onto the toasts and garnish with dill.

MAKES: **12** | PREP TIME: **5 MINS** | COOKING TIME: **10 MINS**

Stuffed Abalone

2 tbsp vegetable oil
2 spring onions (scallions), finely
  chopped, white and green
  parts separated
1 clove of garlic, crushed
1 tsp root ginger, finely grated
12 small live abalone or oysters, shucked
  and half-shells reserved
200 g / 7 oz / 1 ¼ cups jasmine rice,
  cooked and cooled
2 tbsp oyster sauce
1 tsp sesame oil
2 large mild red chillies (chilies),
  finely chopped

1. Heat the vegetable oil in a large wok
   and fry the spring onion, garlic and
   ginger for 2 minutes.
2. Add the abalone and stir-fry for
   2 minutes or until opaque. Remove
   the abalone from the pan and
   roughly chop.
3. Add the rice to the wok and stir-fry
   until piping hot – this should take
   about 4 minutes.
4. Season the rice with oyster sauce and
   sesame oil, then return the abalone
   and stir-fry for 1 minute.
5. Spoon the rice into the reserved
   shells and sprinkle with chilli and
   spring onion greens.
6. Serve immediately.

SERVES: **4** | PREP TIME: **30 MINS** | COOKING TIME: **15 MINS**

Prawn and Vegetable Fried Rice

200 g / 7 oz / 1 ⅓ cups raw king prawns, peeled with tails left intact
2 tbsp yellow bean sauce
30 g dried wood ear fungus
2 tbsp vegetable oil
4 spring onions (scallions), chopped, white and green parts separated
2 cloves of garlic, crushed
1 tbsp root ginger, finely chopped
½ red pepper, deseeded, quartered and sliced
½ yellow pepper, deseeded, quartered and sliced
½ carrot, julienned
200 g / 7 oz / 1 cup canned bamboo shoots, sliced
100 g / 3 ½ oz / ⅔ cup peas, defrosted if frozen
75 g / 2 ½ oz / ⅔ cup beansprouts
500 g / 17 ½ oz / 3 cups long grain rice, cooked and cooled
2 tbsp light soy sauce
2 tsp sesame oil
1 small bunch Chinese chives, cut into short lengths

1. Mix the prawns with the yellow bean sauce and leave to marinate for 30 minutes. Meanwhile, soak the dried fungus in cold water.
2. Heat the vegetable oil in a large wok and fry the spring onion whites, garlic and ginger for 2 minutes. Add the prawns and stir-fry until opaque.
3. Add the vegetables and drained fungus and fry for 4 minutes.
4. Add the rice and stir fry until piping hot – this should take about 4 minutes.
5. Season the rice with soy sauce, sesame oil and black pepper, then serve immediately, garnished with spring onion greens.

SERVES: 4 | **PREP TIME: 15 MINS** | **COOKING TIME: 8 MINS**

Crab and Sweetcorn Soup

400 g / 14 oz / 2 cups canned sweetcorn, drained
1 litre / 1 pint 14 fl. oz / 4 cups chicken or vegetable stock
2 tbsp vegetable oil
4 spring onions (scallions), finely chopped, white parts only
2 tsp fresh root ginger, finely chopped
2 red chillies (chilies), deseeded and chopped
2 tbsp shaoxing rice wine
1 tsp cornflour (cornstarch)
200 g / 7 oz / 1 ⅓ cups fresh white crab meat
1 large egg, beaten
1-2 tbsp light soy sauce

1. Put 150 g of the sweetcorn in a liquidizer with 150 ml of the stock and blend until smooth. Set aside.
2. Heat the oil in a large wok and fry the spring onions, ginger and chillies for 2 minutes. Add the rice wine and cook until evaporated, then pour in the stock and sweetcorn puree.
3. Slake the cornflour with 1 tablespoon of cold water. When the soup starts to boil, pour in the cornflour mixture and stir until thickened.
4. Add the crabmeat and sweetcorn and stir until the soup simmers. Pass the beaten egg through a sieve directly into the soup, stirring to make thin strands of egg.
5. Season the soup to taste with soy sauce and serve immediately.

MAKES: **18** | PREP TIME: **20 MINS** | CHILLING: **30 MINS** | COOKING TIME: **10 MINS**

Seaweed-wrapped Dumplings

350 g / 12 ½ oz / 2 ⅓ cups raw prawns (shrimp), finely chopped
175 g / 6 oz / 1 ¼ cups minced pork
2 spring onions (scallions), finely chopped
2 mild orange chillies (chilies), deseeded and very finely chopped
1 tsp fresh root ginger, finely grated
1 egg white
1 tbsp shaoxing rice wine
1 tbsp cornflour (cornstarch)
3 sheets nori seaweed

1. Mix the prawns with the pork, spring onions, chillies, ginger, egg white, rice wine, and cornflour. Season with 1 tsp salt and some freshly ground white pepper.
2. Lay the nori sheets out on a chopping board, overlapping the seams by 1 cm. Top with the prawn mixture, then roll it up into a tight sausage.
3. Chill the sausage for 30 minutes, then cut it into 2.5 cm (1 in) slices with a very sharp knife.
4. Steam the dumplings for 10 minutes or until opaque in the centre, then serve immediately.

SERVES: 4 | **PREP TIME: 10 MINS** | **MARINATE: 1 HOUR** | **COOKING TIME: 4 MINS**

Spicy Prawn Skewers

1 lime, juiced, plus a few wedges
  to garnish
1 tbsp sriracha chilli sauce
1 clove of garlic, crushed
1 tsp fresh root ginger, finely grated
1 tsp caster (superfine) sugar
1 tbsp light soy sauce
a few sprigs fresh coriander (cilantro),
  finely chopped, plus extra to garnish
12 large raw king prawns, peeled with
  tails left intact

1. Mix the lime juice with the sriracha,
   garlic, ginger, sugar and soy sauce.
   Add the prawns and stir well to coat,
   then cover and marinate in the fridge
   for 1 hour.
2. Meanwhile, soak four wooden
   skewers in cold water for 20 minutes.
3. Thread three prawns onto each
   skewer, then cook under a hot grill for
   2 minutes on each side or until they
   turn pink.
4. Serve immediately, garnished with
   coriander and lime wedges.

Vegetable Dishes
and More

SERVES: 4 | PREP TIME: 5 MINS | COOKING TIME: 10 MINS

Vegetable Fried Rice

2 tbsp vegetable oil
1 small onion, thinly sliced
2 cloves of garlic, crushed
1 tbsp root ginger, finely chopped
2 tsp mixed peppercorns, lightly crushed
1 red romano pepper, deseeded and
thinly sliced
1 Chinese aubergine (eggplant),
quartered and sliced
2 courgettes (zucchini), thinly sliced
500 g / 17 ½ oz / 3 cups long grain rice,
cooked and cooled
2 tbsp light soy sauce
2 tsp sesame oil
2 tbsp pine nuts, toasted
1 tbsp fresh dill, chopped
2 tbsp fresh coriander (cilantro), chopped

1. Heat the vegetable oil in a large wok
   and fry the onion, garlic, ginger
   and peppercorns for 2 minutes.
2. Add the vegetables and fry for
   4 minutes.
3. Add the rice and stir fry until piping
   hot – this should take about 4 minutes.
4. Season the rice with soy sauce and
   sesame oil, then divide between four
   plates and garnish with pine nuts,
   dill and coriander.

Mini Vegetable Spring Rolls

30 g / 1 oz / ½ cup dried shiitake mushrooms
1 tbsp vegetable oil, plus extra to deep fry
1 tsp fresh root ginger, finely chopped
2 clove of garlic, finely chopped
1 carrot, finely julienned
1 red pepper, deseeded and finely julienned
200 g / 7 oz / 1 cup canned bamboo shoots, drained and finely julienned
2 spring onions (scallions), finely julienned
2 Chinese cabbage leaves, finely julienned
1 tsp shaoxing rice wine
1 tsp caster (superfine) sugar
1 tsp cornflour (cornstarch)
1 tbsp light soy sauce
24 wonton wrappers
1 egg white, beaten

1. Soak the mushrooms in cold water for 20 minutes, then drain and finely julienne.
2. Heat 1 tablespoon of vegetable oil in a wok and fry the ginger and garlic for 1 minute. Add the carrot and peppers and stir-fry for 2 minutes. Add the bamboo shoots, spring onions, cabbage and shiitakes and stir-fry for 1 minute.
3. Stir in the wine and sugar, then slake the cornflour in the soy sauce and stir it in. Stir-fry until there is no liquid left in the bottom of the wok. Leave to cool, then chill for 1 hour.
4. Brush the wonton wrappers with egg white, then add a heaped teaspoonful of the mixture to one side of each one. Fold the wanton skin in half and press the edges firmly to seal.
5. Heat the vegetable oil in a deep fat fryer, according to the manufacturer's instructions, to a temperature of 180°C (350F).
6. Fry the spring rolls in batches for 3 minutes or until golden and crisp.
7. Drain on plenty of kitchen paper and serve immediately.

MAKES: 12 | PREP TIME: 30 MINS | COOKING TIME: 3 MINS

Sesame Balls with Red Bean Paste

125 g / 4 ½ oz / ¾ cup muscovado sugar
450 g / 1 lb / 3 cups glutinous rice flour
200 g / 7 oz / 1 cup sweet red bean paste
75 g / 2 ½ oz / ½ cup white sesame seeds
vegetable oil, for deep-frying

1. Dissolve the sugar in 250 ml of boiling water. Sieve the flour into a mixing bowl, then gradually incorporate the sugar water, adding a little extra boiling water if needed to make a pliable dough.
2. Divide the dough into 12 pieces and roll each one into a ball. Flatten the balls and add a spoonful of red bean paste to the centre of each one. Gather up the edges to completely enclose the filling and roll into a neat ball shape again.
3. Dip the balls in a little cold water, then roll in sesame seeds to coat.
4. Heat the oil in a deep fat fryer, according to the manufacturer's instructions, to a temperature of 180°C (350F).
5. Deep fry the balls in batches of three for 3 minutes, or until they turn golden brown and rise to the surface.
6. Drain on plenty of kitchen paper and serve warm.

SERVES: 4 | PREP TIME: 5 MINS | COOKING TIME: 25 MINS

Garlic and Ginger Fried Rice

450 g / 1 lb / 2 ¼ cups long grain rice
2 tbsp vegetable oil
3 cloves of garlic, finely chopped
1 ½ tbsp root ginger, finely chopped
1 tbsp light soy sauce
1 tsp sesame oil

1. Put the rice in a saucepan and add enough water to cover it by 1 cm. Bring the pan to the boil then cover and turn down the heat to its lowest setting.
2. Cook for 10 minutes then turn off the heat and leave to stand, without lifting the lid, for 10 minutes.
3. Heat the vegetable oil in a large wok and fry the garlic and ginger for 1 minute.
4. Add the rice and stir fry for 2 minutes. Season the rice with soy sauce and sesame oil, then serve immediately.

SERVES: 4 | PREP TIME: 20 MINS | COOKING TIME: 5 MINS

Hot and Sour Noodle Soup

300 g / 10 ½ oz wide rice noodles
4 red chillies (chilies), sliced
2 cloves of garlic, chopped
1 tbsp fresh root ginger, chopped
1 tbsp vegetable oil
1 litre / 1 pint 14 fl. oz / 4 cups
  vegetable stock
2 tbsp shaoxing rice wine
2 tsp caster (superfine) sugar
1 lime, juiced
1 tbsp light soy sauce, plus extra to serve
4 lettuce leaves
200 g / 7 oz / 1 ⅓ cups tofu, julienned
½ red onion, sliced
a few sprigs mint

1. Cook the noodles in boiling water according to the packet instructions or until al dente. Plunge into cold water, then drain well and divide between four bowls.
2. Pound three of the chillies in a pestle and mortar with a pinch of salt to a fine paste. Add the garlic and pound again, followed by the ginger.
3. Heat the oil in a large wok and stir-fry the paste for 2 minutes. Add the stock, rice wine, sugar, lime juice and soy sauce and bring to the boil.
4. Ladle the stock over the noodles and garnish each bowl with a lettuce leaf, a pile of tofu, some sliced red onion and chillies and a few sprigs of mint. Serve with extra soy sauce at the table for people to adjust their own seasoning.

SERVES: 4 | PREP TIME: 15 MINS | COOKING TIME: 8 MINS

Tofu and Mushroom Soup

2 red chillies (chilies), sliced
1 clove of garlic, chopped
1 tsp fresh root ginger, chopped
1 litre / 1 pint 14 fl. oz / 4 cups vegetable stock
1 stalk lemongrass, bruised
2 kaffir lime leaves
2 tbsp shaoxing rice wine
2 tsp caster (superfine) sugar
1 tbsp fish sauce
1 lime, cut into 8 wedges
150 g / 5 ½ oz / 2 cups chestnut mushrooms, halved and sliced
3 medium tomatoes, cut into wedges
200 g / 7 oz / 1 ⅓ cups tofu, sliced
holy basil and coriander (cilantro), to garnish

1. Pound three of the chillies in a pestle and mortar with a pinch of salt to a fine paste. Add the garlic and pound again, followed by the ginger.
2. Heat the stock in a large saucepan and dissolve the paste into it. Add the lemongrass, lime leaves, rice wine, sugar and fish sauce and simmer for 5 minutes.
3. Add the lime, mushrooms, tomatoes and tofu and simmer for 3 minutes.
4. Taste the soup and adjust the seasoning with salt, then ladle into bowls and serve, garnished with holy basil and coriander.

SERVES: 4 | **PREP TIME: 5 MINS** | COOKING TIME: **3 MINS**

Choy Sum with Ginger and Spring Onions

3 tbsp vegetable oil
300 g / 10 ½ oz choy sum, trimmed
3 spring onions (scallions), finely julienned
1 tbsp fresh root ginger, finely julienned
1 tbsp sesame oil
2 tbsp light soy sauce

1. Bring a large saucepan of water to the boil and add 1 teaspoon of salt and
   1 tablespoon of the vegetable oil. Blanch the choy sum for 2 minutes, then drain
   well and arrange on a warm serving plate.
2. Top the choy sum with the spring onions and ginger.
3. Heat the rest of the vegetable oil with the sesame oil over a high heat until smoking
   hot, then pour it over the ginger and spring onions.
4. Dilute the soy sauce with 2 tablespoons of boiling water, then pour it over the choy
   sum. Serve immediately.

SERVES: 4 | PREP TIME: 5 MINS | COOKING TIME: 8 MINS

Spicy Vegetable Stir Fry

2 tbsp sesame seeds
2 tbsp vegetable oil
1 red onion, quartered and thinly sliced
3 red chillies (chilies), sliced
2 cloves of garlic, crushed
1 tbsp root ginger, finely chopped
½ tsp ground Szechwan pepper
1 red pepper, deseeded and thinly sliced
1 orange pepper, deseeded and
  thinly sliced
1 Chinese aubergine (eggplant), halved
  and thinly sliced
1 head broccoli, cut into small florets
100 g / 3 ½ oz / 1 cup oyster mushrooms,
  turn into strips
2 tbsp light soy sauce
2 tsp sesame oil
1 handful fresh coriander (cilantro) leaves

1. Dry-fry the sesame seeds in a large wok until lightly toasted, then scrape them into a bowl and set aside.
2. Heat the vegetable oil in the wok and fry the onion, chillies, garlic and ginger for 2 minutes.
3. Sprinkle in the Szechwan pepper, then add the vegetables and fry for 4 minutes.
4. Add the mushrooms and stir-fry for 1 minute, then season with soy sauce and sesame oil.
5. Serve the stir-fry with rice or noodles and sprinkle with the toasted sesame seeds and some coriander leaves.

SERVES: 4 | PREP TIME: 10 MINS | COOKING TIME: 2 MINS

Sesame Seaweed Salad

50 g / 1 ¾ oz / 1 cup dried
  wakame seaweed
1 tbsp sesame seeds
1 tsp Chinese sesame paste
1 tsp runny honey
1 tsp light soy sauce
1 tsp rice wine vinegar

1. Put the dried seaweed in a bowl and cover in hot water. Leave to soak for 5 minutes, then drain well and refresh in cold water. Drain.

2. Dry-fry the sesame seeds in a large wok until lightly toasted, then scrape them into a bowl and set aside.

3. Mix the sesame paste with the honey, soy sauce and vinegar.

4. Toss the seaweed in the dressing and serve sprinkled with sesame seeds.

Wheat Gluten Noodle Soup

300 g / 10 ½ oz wheat noodles
1 litre / 1 pint 14 fl. oz / 4 cups vegetable stock
2 tbsp shaoxing rice wine
2 tbsp light soy sauce
1 tsp caster (superfine) sugar
150 g / 3 ½ oz / 2 cups wheat gluten (rehydrated if dried), cubed
175 g / 6 oz / 2 cups shiitake mushrooms, sliced
3 spring onions (scallions), chopped, green parts only
2 large red chillies (chilies), sliced
2 tsp sesame seeds

1. Cook the noodles in boiling water according to the packet instructions or until al dente. Plunge into cold water, then drain well and divide between four bowls.
2. Heat the stock in a saucepan with the rice wine, soy sauce and sugar. When it starts to boil, add the wheat gluten and shiitakes and simmer for 2 minutes.
3. Ladle the soup over the noodles and serve, garnished with spring onion greens, chillies and sesame seeds.

SERVES: 4 | PREP TIME: 20 MINS

Vegetarian Summer Rolls

6 rice paper wrappers
6 soft lettuce leaves
¼ cucumber, cut into batons
1 carrot, coarsely grated
3 red cabbage leaves, shredded
1 tbsp black and white sesame seeds
edible flowers, to garnish

1. Dip the first rice paper wrapper in a bowl of cold water, then lay it out on a clean chopping board. Lay a lettuce leaf on top and add some cucumber, carrot and cabbage.
2. Fold over the sides of the wrapper, then roll it up to enclose the filling.
3. Repeat with the rest of the ingredients to form six rolls, then cut them into bite-sized pieces. Sprinkle with sesame seeds and serve immediately, garnished with edible flowers.
4. Delicious served as a starter or snack.

SERVES: 4 | PREP TIME: 5 MINS | COOKING TIME: 10 MINS

Spicy Noodles with Spring Onions

400 g / 14 oz medium egg noodles
3 spring onions (scallions), sliced
1 clove of garlic, crushed
50 ml / 1 ¾ fl. oz / ¼ cup chinkiang
(black rice) vinegar
50 ml / 1 ¾ fl. oz / ¼ cup chilli oil
50 ml / 1 ¾ fl. oz / ¼ cup sweet
chilli sauce
2 tbsp light soy sauce

1. Cook the noodles according to the packet instructions, then drain well.
2. Meanwhile, put the spring onions and garlic in a warm serving bowl and whisk in the vinegar, chilli oil, chilli sauce and soy sauce.
3. Toss with the hot noodles and serve immediately.

SERVES: 4 | PREP TIME: 1 HOURS | COOKING TIME: 10 MINS

Shiitake and Glass Noodle Soup

20 small dried shiitake mushrooms
300 g / 10 ½ oz glass noodles
1 tbsp vegetable oil
1 tbsp fresh root ginger, finely chopped
2 tbsp light soy sauce
2 tbsp chinkiang (black rice) vinegar
½ tsp ground white pepper
1 tsp cornflour (cornstarch)
1 tsp sesame oil
3 spring onions (scallions), finely
  chopped, green parts only

1. Cover the shiitake mushrooms in 1.2 litres of boiling water and leave to soak for 1 hour.
2. Meanwhile, cook the noodles in boiling water according to the packet instructions or until al dente. Plunge into cold water, then drain well and divide between four bowls.
3. Remove the mushrooms from the soaking water and dry thoroughly with kitchen paper. Strain the soaking liquor through a muslin-lined sieve and set aside.
4. Heat the vegetable oil in a large wok and fry the ginger for 30 seconds. Add the shiitakes and stir-fry for 2 minutes.
5. Pour in the strained soaking liquor and add the soy sauce, vinegar and white pepper. Slake the cornflour with 1 tbsp of cold water, then stir it into the soup.
6. When the soup simmers and thickens, add the sesame oil and spring onion greens, then taste and adjust the seasoning with salt and white pepper. Ladle over the noodles and serve immediately.

SERVES: 4 | PREP TIME: 45 MINS | COOKING TIME: 5 MINS

Vegetarian Wonton Soup

30 g / 1 oz / ½ cup dried wood ear fungus
½ head broccoli, finely chopped
100 g / 3 ½ oz / ½ cup silken tofu, cut into 5 mm dice
1 tsp fresh root ginger, finely grated
1 tsp shaoxing rice wine
1 tsp caster (superfine) sugar
1 tsp sesame oil
24 wonton wrappers
1 egg white, beaten
1 litre / 17 ½ fl. oz / 4 cups clear vegetable stock
3 baby pak choi, leaves separated
1 tbsp soy sauce

1. Soak the fungus in cold water for 20 minutes, then drain and finely chop.
2. Mix the fungus with the broccoli, tofu, ginger, rice wine, sugar and sesame oil.
   Season with 1 teaspoon of salt and some freshly ground white pepper.
3. Add a teaspoon of the mixture to the centre of each wonton wrapper. Brush round
   the outside with egg white, then draw up the sides of each wrapper and squeeze
   just above the filling to make a sack shape.
4. Bring the vegetable stock to a simmer, then add the wontons and cook for
   2 minutes. Add the pak choi and cook for 2 minutes or until the wontons are tender.
5. Taste the soup and season with soy sauce as necessary. Ladle into four bowls and
   serve immediately.

Steamed Sesame Balls

300 g / 10 ½ oz / 2 cups plain
  (all-purpose) flour
150 g / 5 ½ oz / 1 cup cornflour
  (cornstarch)
75 g / 2 ½ oz / ⅓ cup dark muscovado sugar
1 tsp easy blend dried yeast
50 ml / 1 ¾ fl. oz / ¼ cup sesame oil
2 ½ tsp baking powder
75 g / 2 ½ oz / ½ cup white sesame seeds

1. Mix the flour with the cornflour, sugar and yeast. Stir the oil into 200 ml of warm water, then stir it into the flour.
2. Knead the dough for 10 minutes, then cover and leave to rise for 2 hours.
3. Knead the baking powder into the dough and leave to rest for 15 minutes.
4. Divide the dough into twelve equal balls. Roll each one in sesame seeds to coat, then transfer to a square of greaseproof paper.
5. Steam the buns on the paper squares for 12 minutes, ensuring there's plenty of room for them to expand.
6. Leave to cool a little before serving warm.

Kimchi Fried Rice

2 tbsp vegetable oil
1 small onion, finely chopped
2 cloves of garlic, crushed
1 tbsp root ginger, finely chopped
1 red pepper, deseeded, quartered
  and sliced
200 g / 7 oz / 1 ¾ cups kimchi, chopped
500 g / 17 ½ oz / 3 cups jasmine rice,
  cooked and cooled
2 tbsp light soy sauce
2 tsp sesame oil
1 small bunch Chinese chives, cut into
  short lengths

1. Heat the vegetable oil in a large wok and fry the onion, garlic and ginger for 2 minutes.
2. Add the red pepper and fry for 2 minutes.
3. Add the kimchi and rice and stir fry until piping hot – this should take about 4 minutes.
4. Season the rice with soy sauce, sesame oil and black pepper, then serve immediately, garnished with Chinese chives.

SERVES: 4 | PREP TIME: 20 MINS | COOKING TIME: 25 MINS

Aubergine with Ginger and Spring Onions

2 aubergines (eggplants), cut into
thick batons
2 tbsp vegetable oil
2 tbsp cornflour (cornstarch)
1 tbsp fresh root ginger, cut into a
fine julienne
4 spring onions (scallions), sliced, green
and white parts separated
2 tbsp light soy sauce
1 tsp caster (superfine) sugar
50 ml / 1 ¾ fl. oz / ¼ cup shaoxing
rice wine

1. Dissolve 1 tablespoon of salt in 1 litre
   of water. Add the aubergines and stir
   well, then sit a plate on top to keep
   them submerged. Leave to soak for
   15 minutes, then drain well and
   squeeze dry with plenty of
   kitchen paper.

2. Heat 1 tablespoon of the oil in a large
   wok over a medium heat. Coat the
   aubergine with 1 ½ tablespoons of
   the cornflour, then add a single layer
   of batons to the wok and fry in
   batches until browned all over.
   Transfer finished batches to a plate
   and reserve.

3. Add the rest of the oil to the wok and
   fry the ginger and spring onion whites
   for 2 minutes. Stir the rest of the
   cornflour into the soy sauce, sugar
   and rice wine, then add it to the wok
   and stir for 2 minutes.

4. Add the aubergine batons and stir
   carefully over a medium heat until
   well coated. Spoon into serving bowls
   and serve garnished with the spring
   onion greens.

SERVES: 4 | PREP TIME: 10 MINS | COOKING TIME: 2 MINS

Crispy Seaweed

150 g / 5 ½ oz / 4 ½ cups spring (collared) greens or kale
vegetable oil, for deep frying
1 tsp caster (superfine) sugar
1 pinch five spice powder

1. Remove the tough central veins of the greens, then shred or chop the rest.
2. Blanch the greens in boiling salted water for 1 minute, then drain well. Tip onto a clean tea towel and dry thoroughly. Any leftover moisture will make the oil spit.
3. Heat the oil in a deep fat fryer according to the manufacturer's instructions to a temperature of 180°C (350F).
4. Deep fry the greens in batches for 30 seconds or until crisp, then drain on plenty of kitchen paper.
5. Mix the sugar and five spice with ½ teaspoon of salt and sprinkle it on top of the 'seaweed'.
6. Serve immediately.

SERVES: 4 | PREP TIME: 5 MINS | COOKING TIME: 8 MINS

Egg-fried Rice

2 tbsp vegetable oil
1 clove of garlic, crushed
1 tbsp root ginger, finely chopped
2 spring onions (scallions), chopped
1 large egg
75 g / 2 ½ oz / ½ cup frozen peas, defrosted
1 handful beansprouts
500 g / 17 ½ oz / 3 cups long grain rice, cooked and cooled
1 tbsp light soy sauce
1 tsp sesame oil

1. Heat the vegetable oil in a large wok and fry the garlic, ginger and spring onions for 30 seconds.
2. Add the egg and stir to scramble. Add the peas and beansprouts and stir-fry for 1 minute.
3. Add the rice and stir fry until piping hot – this should take about 4 minutes.
4. Season the rice with soy sauce, sesame oil and black pepper, then serve immediately.

Mushroom Noodle Soup

8 dried shiitake mushrooms
300 g / 10 ½ oz vermicelli rice noodles
1 litre / 1 pint 14 fl. oz / 4 cups
    vegetable stock
2 tbsp shaoxing rice wine
1 tsp caster (superfine) sugar
175 g / 6 oz / 1 ½ cups butternut squash,
    julienned with a mandolin
175 g / 6 oz / 2 cups shimeji mushrooms
¼ leek, thinly sliced
1 handful coriander (cilantro) leaves
chilli bean paste and soy sauce, to serve

1. Cover the shiitake mushrooms in boiling water and leave to soak for 20 minutes.
2. Meanwhile, cook the noodles in boiling water according to the packet instructions or until al dente. Plunge into cold water, then drain well and divide between four bowls.
3. Heat the stock in a saucepan with the rice wine and sugar. Strain the shiitake soaking liquor through a fine sieve and add it to the pan.
4. When it starts to boil, add the squash and simmer gently for 4 minutes or until tender. Scoop it out and divide between the bowls.
5. Add the shimeji to the broth and simmer for 3 minutes. Scoop out and divide between the bowls. Warm through the shiitake in the broth, then add to the bowls and ladle over the stock.
6. Garnish with leek and coriander and serve with chilli bean paste and soy sauce for seasoning at the table.

Egg Chilli Noodles

400 g / 14 oz thin egg noodles
2 tbsp vegetable oil
2 cloves of garlic, crushed
1 tbsp fresh root ginger, finely grated
2 tbsp light soy sauce
4 spring onions (scallions), chopped,
    greens only
3 red chillies (chilies), sliced

1. Cook the noodles in boiling water according to the packet instructions or until al dente, then drain well.
2. Heat the oil in a large wok and fry the garlic and ginger for 1 minute. Add the noodles and stir-fry for 2 minutes, then toss with the soy sauce.
3. Serve immediately, sprinkled with spring onion greens and chillies.

MAKES: 24 | PREP TIME: 45 MINS | COOKING TIME: 10 MINS

Vegetable Dumplings

175 g / 6 oz / 1 ¼ cups plain
    (all-purpose) flour
225 g / 8 oz / 1 ½ cups firm tofu,
    finely diced
1 carrot, coarsely grated
½ red pepper, finely chopped
2 savoy cabbage leaves, deveined and
    finely chopped
2 spring onions (scallions), finely chopped
1 tsp fresh root ginger, finely grated
100 g / 3 ½ oz / ½ cup canned water
    chestnuts, finely chopped
1 tbsp light soy sauce
1 tsp caster (superfine) sugar
1 tsp sesame oil
1 tsp cornflour (cornstarch)
1 egg white, beaten
2 tbsp crab roe (optional)

1. Sift the flour into a bowl and stir in
   160 ml of recently boiled water.
   Knead for 8 minutes or until smooth,
   adding more flour if necessary.
   Rest for 30 minutes.

2. Meanwhile, mix the tofu with the
   carrot, pepper, cabbage, spring
   onions, ginger, water chestnuts,
   soy sauce, sugar, sesame oil and
   cornflour. Season with 1 teaspoon
   of salt and some freshly ground
   white pepper.

3. Divide the rested dough into 24 balls,
   then roll out each one into a 8 cm
   (3 in) circle on a floured surface.

4. Put a heaped teaspoon of filling in the
   centre of each circle, then brush
   round the edge with egg white.
   Gather up the edges and twist round
   to seal.

5. Space out the dumplings in oiled
   steamer baskets and steam for
   10 minutes, then serve immediately.

Index